Bernadette

ANDRÉ RAVIER SJ

Bernadette

With an Introduction by Patrick O'Donovan
Translated by Barbara Wall

Photographs by Helmuth Nils Loose

COLLINS

Published by Collins
London Glasgow
Cleveland New York Toronto
Sydney Auckland Johannesburg

The publishers and photographer wish to thank the following
people:
Mother Marie-Bernadette Gauthey, The Mother Superior, and
Sister Marie-Elisabeth Jean, Superior, of the Convent of Saint
Gildard in Nevers; as well as the Sisters in charge of the Archives
and the Museum; Canon Joseph Bordes, Rector of the Shrines at
Lourdes; Father Ramond, Director of the Press Office for the
Shrines of Lourdes and the Sisters of the Hospice of Lourdes and
of the 'Cachot'. In addition they wish to thank the Directors of
the following museums: The Bernadette Museum and Archives of
Saint Gildard, Nevers; The Bernadette Museum and Archives,
Lourdes.

The author wishes to thank His Eminence Monsignor Jean Streiff,
Bishop of Nevers, who has given his blessing to this work,
published in the hundredth year since the death of Bernadette. He
also wishes to thank Canon Ernest Guynot, Abbé René Laurentin
and Father Michel Olphe-Gailliard and Dom Bernard Billet from
the Benedictine Abbey of Tournay. Finally, he would like to
thank Sister Marie-Thérèse Bourgeade for her tireless work in
helping to prepare this volume.

Imprimi potest
Jean Streiff, Bishop of Nevers
Nevers, 7 October 1978

Original edition © Verlag Herder Freiburg im Breisgau 1979
First published in Great Britain 1979
UK ISBN 0-00-216187-7
First published in the USA 1979
USA ISBN 0-529-05672-0
Library of Congress Catalog Card Number 79-51569
Made and printed in Great Britain by
William Collins Sons & Co Ltd, Glasgow

Contents

Preface

'It is more moving to read the Passion than to have it exp. .d', declared Bernadette some days before her death. It is this remark that has inspired the presentation of this book: as often as possible we have left it to Bernadette to speak, and even the illustrations keep close to the essentials. In fact Bernadette's 'passion', a passion illumined by her faith in the Resurrection, cannot be expounded or 'explained', to use her word. We have to see her living, we have to see her descending step by step, like Christ (*Phil*. 2: 6–11), right to the depths of human weakness, while uniting herself to the love of the Father who is in Heaven. If we were asked to define her spiritual way, we would say, quite simply, it was living – both in her personal experience and in the thick texture of existence – what had been given to her, as to every Christian, at baptism: union with Jesus crucified and Jesus risen.

This is why we could say, following St Paul's words, that God gave her a name not higher than all other names but among the names of his greatest friends.

Bernadette, a saint of our race, carnal and spiritual.

A. RAVIER

Introduction

Christians, Moslems, Jews and Hindus all have holy places. These are places where the supernatural is believed to have struck the earth like a bolt of lightning. Catholics have had hundreds of these, with Rome and Jerusalem standing as the rocks of their foundation. But after these came the shrines of the Virgin Mother of God, which signify the love and gentleness and hope which should be the great outward sign of their faith. Their very failure to exhibit these qualities has made these shrines the more desperately important.

There was ancient Ephesus – lost now in Turkey – where Mary may have died. There is Loreto and Walsingham and Guadalupe and Fatima and Knock. And all of them, unlike many other revered shrines, are almost devoid of any political or national implications. But the most universal of them all, the one to which the Catholic world beats a popular and teeming and quite classless path, is Lourdes. Except for its setting, it is not even beautiful. The vulgarity of its corrupt commercial quarter is strident. And yet this does not matter.

This is the great international shrine of Our Lady. It has become a powerhouse of prayer and emotion. Its claims to miracles are controlled with a dauntingly professional and clinical care. And what brought this all about has been recorded and documented as carefully as if some great State crime had been committed at the grotto of Massabielle.

It must be remembered that this happened in the Second Empire, the 'gaslit' Empire of Napoleon III. Police and Church authorities, not wholly in sympathy with each other, kept meticulous and almost neurotically suspicious records. We know a great deal about what happened in this mountain town in the foothills of the Pyrenees in 1858. It has all been elaborately recorded and sometimes interpreted most beautifully by writers. But the passive recipient of the vision, the heroine and the victim of Lourdes seldom gets more than the equivalent of a walking-on part. She is a spear carrier in this drama or miracle of Our Lady and this is precisely the role that she would have chosen.

Bernadette Soubirous has been set on one side as a lumpish and ignorant peasant and it is true that her ignorance of the meaning of, 'I am the Immaculate Conception', even in her own *patois*, was part of the evidence for something that could be no fraud. She has been made innocuous and unattractive, an innocent saint whose life was as unsophisticated and spiritually unexciting as the statue of Our Lady of Lourdes set up in the Grotto.

But André Ravier has written in the spiritual life of this girl who is now a canonized saint of the Roman Church. She apparently was chosen for a visual and auditory experience far more realistic and proveable than anything that happened to St Theresa of Avila or St Theresa of Lisieux. And whereas in the Theresas, the Eagle and the Dove, the dominant and intellectual and fastidious lady, as great and literate as any in Europe, and the other as nobly humble and percipient as any saint, are of special interest to Catholic intellectuals in search of stability in religious and physical pain, St Bernadette has achieved no such status.

It is deadly difficult to write the life story of a saint who is both a very private person and who consciously avoids too much self-expression, if only because to do that would be to engage in a certain pride. Yet this book is the life of, especially the spiritual life of Saint Bernadette Soubirous. And here in photographs and popular prints are the evidence of her times. She becomes a figure of the history of our time, a well authenticated news story.

After her experience, she went into a convent where the reality of the nineteenth century class system seemed to prevail and to act especially upon an underprivileged girl who has seen a vision that had been approved of by the ecclesiastical authorities. She experienced the serenities and the irritations of the cloisters. She took her reprimands. She could be tetchy. She got no reward on earth. She even agonized to her end over the small details of her depositions to the Church and the State and she died young and after a long agony of pain. But she also left what we would call commonplace books as well as letters and statements that show the uttermost in an attempted abandonment to God. She may have been an inelegant and muddy peasant girl with a quarrelsome family; she became by training, suffering and conscious acceptance one of the great ladies in the hierarchy of history and heaven.

PATRICK O'DONOVAN

Lourdes, Early February, 1858

The winter nights fall quickly in the narrow little street of Petits-Fossés. And faster still in the cell of the former prison with windows giving onto a walled courtyard. Here it is that François and Louise Soubirous and their four children now live, and what is there to do in this damp darkness but stretch out on the two beds – relics of better days – and try to sleep till dawn?

But before going to bed the Soubirous say their prayers. They did so in the happy days at the mill at Boly (1842–54), they did so wherever their moves took them, and they do so now in the cell. François and Louise draw their children together before the crucifix hanging on the wall. Each makes the sign of the cross and Bernadette, being the eldest, starts the family prayers.

The prayers in the cell are neither long nor complicated. They are the prayers of simple Christians: *Our Father, Hail Mary, I Believe.* Indeed Bernadette knows no others; with great patience she has managed to memorize these, and sometimes as she says them she slips the beads of her 'little tuppenny rosary' through her fingers; she keeps it in the pocket of her pinafore. A detail not without importance: at the end of prayers they invoke 'Mary, conceived without sin', a devotion popularized among churchgoers by the promulgation of the dogma of the Immaculate Conception in 1854.

And this is just about all, but it is a great deal.

Our Father . . . there is someone who loves us in spite of, or because of, our poverty, someone who does not reject us, someone who opens his heart to us when all the doors of Lourdes are closed.

Thy will be done . . . yes, that disconcerting will, the will which in 1854 took us from our happy mill at Boly to the Laborde house, then in 1855 took us from there to the little farm at Arcizac, then early in 1856 back to Lourdes again, to a single room in the Ribes-Soubies house, then in May of that same year to this damp hovel once used for prisoners; the will which has allowed me, François Soubirous, an honest miller by trade, to become a casual labourer.

Give us this day our daily bread . . . a little rye bread so that all of us can survive, and a bit of white bread for the frail stomach of our eldest . . . *Deliver us from evil* . . . *Lead us not into temptation,* temptation to jealousy, hate, blasphemy, revolt . . . Rather, *forgive us our trespasses,* for we too are sinners.

Hail Mary . . . how good it is to greet you as a Mother, to bless you, you to whom Our Lord said Mother so that as *Mother of God* you would also be our Mother . . . So, *pray for us*, you know better than we do what we need . . . *now*, today, and also tomorrow, so heavy with anxieties, and *at the hour of our death* . . . death which has already taken two of our children, and nearly took Bernadette, of cholera, two years ago . . . death which hangs over the heads of all of us.

François and Louise must think of all those things while they pray.

And Bernadette? Bernadette is fourteen at this time and looks younger, but she has great strength of character, great clarity of vision, great perseverance. Life has already matured her. From many points of view this child is already a woman. She was ten in 1854 when her parents left the mill at Boly, where she had been happy, although two little brothers had died. Since that time she has, as the eldest, shared in her parents' worries, griefs, humiliations. She has known illness, suffering, hunger. She is aware of her ignorance, of her 'backwardness' – at fourteen she cannot yet read and write. How could she have gone to school like other little girls, like her sister Toinette, when she had to look after her little brothers all the time while her mother was out working as a daily cleaner? She is probably unaware of the word 'humility' and yet she practises it, and she faces life with faith in God, *Our Father*, and in *Mary*, *his Mother*. She has the courage of the poor who know that they have only their arms and their heads to count on. One day she said to her cousin, Jeanne Védère (this is the only authentic remark from her childhood that we have): 'When God permits something, we don't complain,' which is a translation, at her level, of *Thy will be done*.

Recently, on account of her health, Bernadette has been staying with a family in the country, in Bartrès, looking after children and sheep, but she returned to Lourdes last month so as to be able to prepare for her First Communion. She finds it very difficult to learn her catechism. But when the day of her First Communion arrives, she will have learnt about the knowledge of God better than any book could have taught her.

II *At Massabielle*

11 February 1858. The First Appearance: Familiarisation

It all began because of their poverty. There was no wood in the prison cell where they lived, none for warming themselves and none for cooking their meagre meal. There was only one solution, to go out into the fields and collect twigs and branches from under the trees, and with a little luck there might be some bones, too, which they could sell to old Pigou for a few pennies.

So Bernadette, her sister Toinette and their friend Jeanne Abadie, known as Baloum, set off light-heartedly along the Pont Vieux road. Here is Bernadette's account of what happened:

'The first time I went to the grotto was Thursday, 11 February 1858. I was going to collect wood with two other children along the banks of the Gave. When we arrived at the mill' – that is to say the Savy mill whose wheels were turned by a small tributary of the Gave – 'I asked the other children if they would like to go and see where the mill stream joined the Gave. They said yes. So we followed along the stream.

'When we arrived there' – that is, at the end of the tongue of sand and shingle formed by the confluence of the Gave and the stream, just opposite the grotto called Massabielle, meaning the ancient mass – 'we found ourselves in front of a grotto.

'As we could go no further, my two companions set out to cross the water in front of the grotto.

'When they had crossed it, they started to cry. I was alone on the other side' – that is to say on the tongue of sand and shingle. 'I asked them why they were crying. They said the water was cold. I asked them to help me throw some stones into the water so that I could make my way across without taking off my shoes and stockings' – Bernadette had suffered from a painful form of asthma ever since having cholera in 1855. 'The only answer thay gave me was to tell me to do as they had done. So I went a little further on to see if I could cross without taking off my shoes and stockings. But I couldn't.

'So I returned to the place opposite the grotto and started taking off my shoes and stockings. Hardly had I taken off the first stocking than I heard a noise, as if there was a rush of wind.' Bernadette was sometimes to describe it as a 'roar'.

'Then I looked over towards the fields and saw that the trees there were not moving at all. I went on taking off my shoes and stockings. I heard the same noise again.

'I raised my head and looked towards the grotto. I saw a Lady dressed in white, wearing a white dress, a blue girdle and a yellow rose on each foot, the same colour as the chain of her rosary: the beads of her rosary were white.'

This phenomenon was enough to astonish and even to frighten Bernadette. Yet everything was to unfold in such a way as to soften the initial shock and give Bernadette security, peace and joy. She on her side would do all she could to verify the reality of what she had seen. As for the Lady, she would be nothing but smiles, goodness and beauty; she would make herself familiar.

'The Lady signed to me to approach; but I was frightened; I dared not move; I thought I had made some mistake; I rubbed my eyes, but it was no use. I looked again and I still saw the same Lady.

'Then I put my hand in my pocket and took out my rosary.

'I wanted to make the sign of the cross, but I couldn't; I couldn't lift my hand to my forehead, it fell back again. Then I became more frightened than ever and yet I couldn't move.

'The Lady took the rosary which she held in her hands and made the sign of the cross. My hand was trembling. Then I started not being frightened; I took my rosary again; I tried to make the sign of the cross too and this time I could; and as soon as I had made it, I was calm, the great fear which I had felt left me. I knelt down and said my rosary, always having this beautiful Lady before my eyes. The vision ran the beads of hers between her fingers but she did not move her lips.

'When I had finished my rosary, the Lady beckoned me to approach her, but I didn't dare; I stayed exactly where I was.

'Then the vision suddenly disappeared.'

It was over. No word had been exchanged between the Lady and Bernadette; but contact had been established.

What would Bernadette do? She simply rejoined Toinette and Baloum who were busy collecting wood and also any old bones that the Gave might have washed up into the grotto. The two little girls had been aware of Bernadette on her knees – well, she was welcome to pray given that she did not want to cross the water. And time was pushing on. They had already heard the church bell ringing the angelus.

'I took off my other stocking,' so Bernadette's account goes on, 'so as to cross the little strip of water in front of the grotto and join my companions.'

Soon three bundles of firewood had been tied up. 'And we went away.' Now that the Lady was no longer there, Bernadette was left to her perplexity. 'As we walked along, I asked my companions whether they has seen anything. "No," they said . . . I asked them again, and again they said that they had seen nothing.'

But Toinette and Baloum had been intrigued by Bernadette's insistence. '"Why, did you see anything?" they asked. "Oh no! If you didn't see anything, neither did I." I didn't want to tell them about it, I was afraid I had been mistaken.'

Silence. But the curiosity of the two little girls had been aroused. 'All the way home, they asked me what I had seen. As they couldn't leave the subject alone, I decided to tell them, but on condition that they wouldn't tell anyone. They promised to keep the secret. Then they told me that I ought not to go back there; I said no. Then they said that they wouldn't either, for they believed it was someone who wanted to harm us.

'As soon as they were home, they made haste to tell the story at once, that I had seen a Lady dressed in white.

'That was the first time.'

On hearing Toinette's account Louise, her mother, was troubled. And so was her father, François. They had quite enough worries at home as it was! What was this new story? Bernadette was forbidden to return to the grotto.

On Saturday evening Bernadette went to find Father Pomian in his confessional – the priest who was preparing the children for their first Communion. 'I saw something white which resembled a Lady,' she told him through the grill, and she recounted all that had happened at Massabielle. He prudently asked his 'penitent', whom he hardly knew, to dispense him from keeping the secret of the confessional so that he could discuss the matter with the parish priest of Lourdes, Father Peyramale.

Sunday, 14 February. The Second Appearance: The Holy Water Test

It was Sunday. On coming out of High Mass, Toinette, Baloum and a few other companions gathered round Bernadette: 'Let's go to the grotto!' Bernadette asked for nothing better, but her parents had forbidden it.

'The second time was the following Sunday. I went back there because I felt urged to in my inmost self. My mother had forbidden me to go there. After High Mass, the two other little girls and myself asked my mother again. Again she said no.

'She told me she was afraid I would fall into the water; she was afraid I wouldn't be back in time for vespers. I promised her that I would be. So she allowed me to go.

'I went into church to get a small bottle of holy water so as to throw it at the vision when I reached the grotto, if I saw it.

'When we arrived there, each of us took out our rosary, and we knelt down to say it. Hardly had I said the first decade than I saw the same Lady. So then I started throwing the holy water at her, while telling her, if she came from God, to stay, and, if not, to go. Then she smiled, and bowed; and the more I sprinkled her with water, the more she smiled and bowed her head, and the more I saw her making signs. Then suddenly I was very frightened and quickly threw all the water at her until my bottle was finished. Then I went on saying my rosary.

'She disappeared, and we went away to go to vespers.'

Again silence on the part of the Lady. Yet one thing was certain, the vision was not the devil: if so the holy water would have put it to flight! So, what was it?

Thursday, 18 February. The Third Appearance: Invitation to a Meeting

'The third time was the following Thursday. The Lady did not speak to me until the third time. I went to the grotto with some grownups' – Madame Milhat and Antoinette Peyret – 'who advised me to take paper and ink and to ask her, if she had anything to say to me, to be so good as to write it down.

'When we arrived at the grotto, I started as usual to say my rosary; hardly had I said a few Hail Maries than I had the same vision. I said to the Lady the words [I had been told to say]. She smiled and said that what she had to tell me need not be written down, but she asked me if I would be gracious enough to go there every day for a fortnight.

Louise and François Soubirous, Bernadette's parents

The mill at Boly where Bernadette was born on 7 January 1844 and where she spent a happy childhood until 1854

An entry in the parish register of Lourdes marks the baptism of Marie Bernadette Soubirous on 9 January 1844

Font in the former parish church of Lourdes

A room in the house of Bernadette's nurse in Bartrès

The 'cachot' at Lourdes, where the Soubirous family found accommodation in May 1856

A photo of Bernadette taken c. 1861, when Bernadette lived with the Sisters in the Hospice of Lourdes

Father Peyramale of Lourdes, to whom Bernadette repeated the instruction of the 'Lady' and on 25 March 1858 the words 'I am the Immaculate Conception'

The Grotto of Massabielle in its original condition. A photo taken in 1858. Bernadette stood by the white block of stone in front of the Grotto when she saw the 'Lady' for the first time

Stones in the bed of the River Gave opposite the Grotto of Massabielle

Bernadette in the Grotto. A photograph taken in 1864 by the photographer Lacaze.

Copie page 69

1er Original du Récit de la main de Bernadette écrit par elle même en 1866

grotte de Lourdes

La première fois que je fut à a grotte j'allais rammasser du bois avec deux autres petites, quand nous fûmes au moulin nous suivîmes le canal pour voir ou elles allait se rejoindre avec le gave, elles me repondirent que oui. La première fois que je fus à la grotte j'allais rammassai du bois avec deux autres petites filles, quand nous fûmes au moulin je leur demandé si elles voulait aller voirs où bien du moulin allez se joinire au gave, elles me repondirent oui, à la nous suivîmes le canal et nous nous trouvâmes devans une grotte ne pouvent allez plus loing, mes deux compagnes se mirent en même de traverser l'eau qui a trouve devans la grotte, comme je me trouai seule de l'autre coté, j'ai demandé aussi tres deux, si elles voulait m'ôter à jeter quelques pierres dans l'eau pour voir si je pourai passer sans me dechoser elles me dirent de faire comme elles si je voulais, je fus un peu plus loing voir ou je pourais passer sans me dechoser mais inutilement. alors je revint de vans la grotte et je mêmes à me dechoser a peine si j'avais ôté le premier bas, j'entendis un bruit comme comme un coup de vans alors j'ai tourné la tête du coté de la prairie j'ai vue les arbres très calmes alors je continuai de me dechoser j'entendis encore le même bruit comme je leut la tête et en regardant la grotte, j'apercu une Dame en blanc, alors je fus un peu saisi, et croyant être en face d'une ilusion je me frotai les yeux

Handwritten account by Bernadette of the appearances in the Grotto. Archives of the Convent of Saint Gildard in Nevers

'I answered that I would.'

This is the place to point out that Bernadette referred to the 'vision' or the 'Lady' as 'Aquerò' (meaning 'it') up till 25 March when the Lady revealed her name; and also that 'Aquerò', during her appearances, addressed Bernadette in the Lourdes dialect, not in French. Her voice, according to the girl who heard it, was 'sweet and gentle'.

Bernadette's accounts of the first three appearances as given in the manuscripts are very full when compared with the few lines which she devotes to the message given her by the Lady during the fortnight's meetings. A more important factor is that the various elements of the message – the words, the gestures – are not recounted in the same order in the different manuscript versions, and this makes the accurate dating of some of these elements very difficult, if not impossible. To make matters worse, some of Aquerò's words – according to Bernadette's formal evidence – were said to her 'several times'. The result is that historians have taken divergent views in their reconstruction of events. In his masterly study of the 'appearances', Father R. Laurentin has patiently unravelled the tangled threads of the skein as far as this was possible, and his analysis reveals that Bernadette suffered from a 'memory-block' – such a serious one that, if we relied on certain manuscripts, we would get the impression that most of the things that were said to her in the fortnight were said initially at the third appearance! This memory-block is obvious and it shows itself right from Bernadette's earliest accounts. On the other hand Bernadette provides accounts of certain events during the 'fortnight' which, for precision of detail, yield nothing to the accounts of the first two appearances. So what conclusions can we draw? Perhaps the key to the problem lies in the relationship that always exists between the memory of an event and the interest it arouses. What Bernadette remembered from the 'fortnight' was first and foremost the words that made up the message: they seemed to her more important than this or that detail, so she reports them with the same sobriety, vivacity and precision as she displayed when reporting the Lady's name to Father Peyramale on 25 March – the date on which the name was revealed to her. If this is the correct interpretation, then Bernadette would have experienced a shift of interest away from external circumstances and towards the very words of the message.

However this may be, it seems that it is to the third appearance – that of 18 February – that we unquestionably owe Aquerò's utterance: 'I do not promise to make you happy in this world, but in the other.'

19 February – 4 March.
The Fortnight of Appearances

'I went back to the grotto every day for a fortnight. The vision appeared every day, with the exception of one Monday and one Friday.

'She told me several times that I should tell the priests that a chapel should be built there and that I should go to the fountain' – the spring – 'to wash myself and that I should pray for the conversion of sinners. In the space of this fortnight she gave me three secrets which she forbade me to tell anyone. I have been faithful so far.'

Among the events of the fortnight, some stood out in lasting relief in Bernadette's memory: the discovery of the spring, the interrogations she underwent from Police Inspector Jacomet and the public prosecutor Dutour, and her 'mission' to Father Peyramale. This is how she describes them:

Police Inspector Jacomet

'On the first Sunday of the fortnight, as I was coming out of church' – it was after vespers – 'a local official' – it was the *garde champêtre* Collet – 'took me by the hood and told me to follow him. I followed him and, on the way, he told me that they would send me to prison. I listened in silence and we arrived at the police station. The police inspector took me into a room alone with him, gave me a chair, and I sat down. Then he took some paper and told me to recount what had happened at the grotto. I did so. After having written a few lines which I had dictated, he added other things that were strange to me. Then he said he would read back what he had written to see if he had made any mistakes, so I listened carefully. But after he had read a few lines there were mistakes, so I said sharply: I didn't say that, sir. Then he became angry and said yes, I did, and I again said no. This argument lasted for a few minutes; and when he saw that he was mistaken and that I persisted in telling him that I hadn't said that, he went a little further on and started again to read what I had never said and I went on insisting that it was not so. The same things were said over and over again. I was there for an hour or an hour and a half. Every now and again I heard kicks at the door and banging at the windows and men's voices shouting: "If you don't let her out we shall break down the door."

'When the time came for me to go, the police inspector accompanied me, opened the door, and there I saw my father who was waiting impatiently with a crowd of other people who had followed me from church. That was the first time that I was obliged to appear before those Gentlemen.'

By good fortune the notes of Jacomet's interrogations have been preserved. What they say, and in particular their erasures, confirm the accuracy of Bernadette's account: she had known very well how to avoid the traps and dishonest questions that are customary in this sort of interrogation, although Jacomet, by his physical presence and the prestige of his office, might well have overawed 'the little Soubirous'. In fact she was laughing as she emerged from her ordeal. 'What are you laughing at?' people asked, and she said 'He was trembling. He had a tassel on his cap that tinkled.'

The Spring

The 'discovery' of the spring is difficult to date. All the historians agree that it was between 22 and 27 February but they differ as to the exact day. We shall align ourselves with Father Laurentin and opt for 25 February.

'The Lady told me that I must go and drink at the spring and wash myself there. As I didn't see any spring, I went to drink in the Gave. The Lady told me that it wasn't there; she signed to me with her finger to look beneath the rock. I went and there I found a trickle of water resembling mud, but there was so little of it that I could hardly collect any in the hollow of my hand. I obeyed, however, and started scratching; after that, I was able to collect some. I threw it away three times because it was so dirty; at the fourth time I was able to drink it.

'She also told me to eat a plant which grew in the same place as where I drank; just once, I don't know why.' When someone said to her later that this was a very foolish thing to do, she replied: 'But we eat salad.'

'Then the vision disappeared and I departed.'

There is one thing that surprises everyone familiar with the manuscript accounts of the appearances. Nowhere does Bernadette write the word 'penance'. On the contrary, it is always a matter of 'praying for sinners'. Would not Aquerò have uttered the word 'penance'? Yes, Bernadette's oral accounts and the stories of witnesses are categorical. In any case the actions that Aquerò indicated several times to Bernadette, such as washing at the spring, advancing along the ground on her knees, kissing the ground, had a significance which did not escape her. To anyone who asked her why the Lady had told her to eat some leaves from that plant growing along the damp fringe of the spring, she answered simply: 'For sinners.' Prayer and penance went side by side in her eyes when it was a matter of converting sinners.

The Public Prosecutor

It was probably on the evening of that same day, 25 February, that the public prosecutor, Dutour, summoned Bernadette to his office. François Soubirous was away, so Louise accompanied her daughter. Once in the presence of this important personage, Louise was nervous, but Bernadette no more so than when before the police inspector. Indeed it was not long before the girl had taken the advantage over the magistrate. The notes copied by Dutour into his reports for 1878–9 confirm the accuracy of the account of the interview left by Bernadette.

'The second time it was with the public prosecutor. That same week the inspector sent the same official [*the garde champêtre*] to tell me to be at the public prosecutor's at six o'clock. I went there with my mother. Then he asked me what had happened at the grotto. I told him everything and he wrote it down. Afterwards he read it back to me, as the police inspector had done, that is to say he had written down some things which I never said. So I said: I didn't say that, sir. But he said yes, I did, and for answer all I could say was no. Finally, after having argued enough, he admitted his mistakes, and continued to read, but he always made fresh mistakes, telling me that he had the inspector's notes and it wasn't the same story. I assured him that I had told him the same story, and that if the inspector was mistaken it was so much the worse for him. Then he told his wife to send someone to fetch the inspector and some petty official to take me to spend the night in prison. My poor mother had been crying for some time now; she looked at me now and again, and when she heard that they were going to put us in prison, her tears fell in greater abundance. I tried to console her by saying: You are quite right to cry because we're going to prison, for we have done no wrong to anyone. Then he offered us chairs at the moment of going out to wait for the answer. My mother took one, for she was all trembling after standing for two hours. As for me I thanked the prosecutor and sat on the floor like a tailor.

'There were some men round about who were watching what was going on, and when they saw that we never came out they started kicking at the door: although the petty official was there, he could do nothing to control them. Now and again the prosecutor put his head to the window to tell them not to make so much noise, but they told him to let us out or else they'd go on and on. Then he decided to let us out, saying that the inspector was too busy and that the matter was put off until the next day.'

The prosecutor was not wearing a cap with a tassel that tinkled, but his

Right Old sheepfold in Bartrès, where Bernadette lived with her nurse Marie Laguës and worked as a shepherdess during 1857–8

hand shook, he missed the hole of his inkwell when he wanted to dip his pen, and he scribbled his notes tirelessly. None of this escaped Bernadette's notice. 'When people don't write well,' she asked as she came out of Dutour's room, 'do they make crosses? The prosecutor was always making crosses.'

The self-possession and presence of mind displayed by Bernadette when she appeared before her judges, or when cunning or sceptical visitors cross-questioned her, fills us with amazement. And she herself was surprised. Later, when she was at Nevers, she admitted to Sister Vincent Garros: 'There was something in me that enabled me to rise above everything; I was tackled from all sides, but nothing mattered, I wasn't afraid.'

The mission to Father Peyramale and Aquerò's real name: 25 March
Was it 'the third time', that is to say on 18 February (as many manuscripts would have us believe), that the Lady of Massabielle asked Bernadette to 'tell the priests to build a chapel there' and even 'to go there in procession'? It seems likely that the phenomenon of 'memory-block' came into play here. Be that as it may, Bernadette's 'mission' to the parish priest of Lourdes, Father Peyramale, developed over the fortnight's meetings; several times during this period she transmitted Aquerò's demands to the parish priest and his questions back to Aquerò. Until 25 March 1858 when Aquerò at last disclosed her name.

It was no small thing for Bernadette to present herself before Father Peyramale. Clothed in an imposing cassock, this giant of a man was an intimidating person, and when he spoke from the pulpit his harsh booming voice made the whole parish tremble. Yet he was the nicest man in the world. When Bernadette went the first time with a message from Aquerò she took her aunts Bernarde and Basile with her – a somewhat nervous bodyguard, for not only did Father Peyramale inspire fear in all his parishioners, but these two had on their conscience various youthful misdemeanours that had been reported abroad. At the very idea of a procession the priest reacted in so severe a manner that Bernadette forgot to mention the chapel. So she returned to the presbytery that night. Aunts Bernarde and Basile managed to escape this visit, and it was Dominquette Cazenave who accompanied Bernardette to this second interview.

'I went to see the parish priest to tell him that a Lady had ordered me to tell the priests to build a chapel in that place. He looked at me for a moment, and then he said in a rather discouraging voice: "Who is this Lady?" I replied that I didn't know. So he told me to ask her her name

Left The so-called 'blue portrait' of Bernadette by Du Roure in the Museum of Lourdes

and come back and tell him what it was. The next day, when I arrived at the grotto, and after saying my rosary, I asked her her name on behalf of the priest, but she only smiled. On my return I went to the priest and told him that I had done what he said but that she had given no answer except a smile. Then he told me that she was making fun of me and that I would do better not to go back any more, but I couldn't help going.

'I went every day for a fortnight, and each time I asked her who she was, which always made her smile.'

At the end of the fortnight the question of the chapel seemed to have come to a dead end. However, Bernadette had scrupulously fulfilled her mission: at least three times she had been to the parish priest and told him of Aquerò's demand. But Father Peyramale on his side had dug in his heels; in order to believe the message he required that the Lady should tell her name and give a sign: 'Let her make the rosebush in the grotto bloom,' he said. For a rosebush at Lourdes to bloom in early March would indeed be a miracle! Bernadette transmitted the parish priest's latest idea to the Lady. Silence and a smile. On 4 March, when the fortnight came to an end, that was how matters stood.

Now that the fortnight had come to an end, Bernadette was liberated from her promise to the Lady, so she obeyed her parish priest and her parents, stopped going to the grotto and went back to school instead. Everything seemed to have come to an end. Then, suddenly, at dawn on the Feast of the Annunciation, everthing flared up again. Bernadette felt 'urged' by the inner compulsion she knew so well to go down to the grotto. At five o'clock in the morning there she was hurrying towards Massabielle.

The Lady was already there. When the rosary was finished, she stepped lightly from the hollow above to the ground below where she was on the same level as the group praying around the visionary. Bernadette had not yet resigned herself to the failure of her mission concerning the chapel, so she took up the question from where she had left it three weeks ago.

'When I went after the fortnight I asked her three times in succession who she was. She smiled as usual. Finally I ventured to ask a fourth time. With her two arms hanging down, she raised her eyes and looked up at the sky, and it was then that she told me, joining her hands together now at the height of her breast, that she was the Immaculate Conception. Those were the last words she ever said to me.

'Then I went again to the parish priest to tell him that she was the Immaculate Conception, and he asked me if I was really sure. I answered yes and that, so as not to forget the phrase, I had said it over to myself all the way home.'

These closing lines of Bernadette's account, so simple, so bare, must be very carefully considered.

'Immaculate Conception'? Bernadette was always to stumble when saying those words whose meaning was unknown to her. And when she wrote them down she hesitated over the spelling. Had she ever heard them before? Of course she knew that at church there had been for some time a chapel dedicated to the Virgin Mary's conception; and then, on 4 March 1855, the priests had read in all the churches of the diocese of Tarbes Pope Pius IX's encyclical proclaiming Mary as 'immaculate in her conception'. But there is a great gulf between 'to hear' and 'to understand' particularly when a mystery is in question. Moreover Aquerò's formula was strange: I am the Immaculate Conception. What could that really have represented to Bernadette? And even to Father Peyramale, to his curates and indeed to theologians? In order to grasp such a formula we have almost to refer back to Christ's phrase in the Gospel: 'I am the Resurrection.' This identification of a person with one of his mysteries could legitimately be disconcerting, that is to say it could either shock or dazzle according to the case. We can understand why Father Peyramale asked Bernadette if she was 'really sure' that was the name; and we can understand even better why Bernadette had to repeat it all the way home!

This name was worth considerably more than any number of roses on a rosebush in winter. Father Peyramale became convinced: he became, as from that day, one of Bernadette's most zealous defenders. As for the messenger herself, the appearance that took place on 25 March impressed her to the deepest fibres of her being. In later years she was often asked to reproduce the Virgin Mary's gestures and repeat her words, and then a sort of radiance would possess and transfigure her. When in 1863 Fabisch, the famous Lyonese sculptor, was entrusted with the difficult task of carving the statue of the Immaculate Conception for the grotto, he asked Bernadette to reproduce the scene. 'Bernadette,' so he recorded, 'stood up with great simplicity, then joined her hands and raised her eyes to heaven. I have never seen anything so beautiful.' And yet when she was shown his statue, Bernadette said, as she said of all the other statues of the Virgin, 'No, that's not it at all!'

The Appearance of 7 April:
The Seal is Set by a Miracle

The Blessed Virgin appeared twice more to Bernadette.

On 7 April, the Wednesday in Easter week, Bernadette heard the familiar call within her and before dawn was in ecstasy in front of the grotto. A large crowd had accompanied her. And then there occurred a miracle equivalent to the blooming of roses on the rosebush of Massabielle: a miracle which, as it were, set God's seal on the appearances. In front of some thousand witnesses who were thronging around her, the flame of a large candle burnt through Bernadette's fingers without her flesh being affected. Doctor Dozous, who had come there as an expert to verify the phenomenon of ecstasy, forbade anyone to intervene during this happening or to remove the visionary's hands from the candle. Holding his watch, he recorded that ten minutes had passed in this manner. Then, still in ecstasy, Bernadette took hold of her candle in the normal way. When the ecstasy was over, Doctor Dozous examined the visionary's hands very carefully. 'There's nothing,' he declared, 'nothing.' Previously he had been sceptical about the appearances; now he believed.

On 3 June, the feast of Corpus Christi, Bernadette made her first Communion. Various pieces of information have come down to us concerning that very personal event. One comes from Father Peyramale. He wrote to the Bishop of Tarbes that during the preparatory retreat, which he himself gave for the children, Bernadette 'was as recollected and attentive as could possibly be desired'. On the day of the first Communion itself, 'she appeared to be steeped in the holy act she was performing.' and he added: 'Everything is developing within her in an astonishing way.' Astonishing perhaps, but simple and ordinary and in accordance with the faith of all baptized people who are conscious of what their baptism is. We are already in the presence of the secret of Bernadette's deep spiritual life. She gives us a momentary glimpse of the joy of her first Communion by this confidence to Emmanuélite Estrade who asked her the following day: 'Tell me, Bernadette, which made you happier, receiving Our Lord or talking to the Blessed Virgin in the grotto?' She replied: 'I don't know, the two things go together and cannot be compared. What I do know is that I was very happy in both of them.'

Our Lord said to his Father: 'I give you thanks for having revealed these things to the little ones.'

Bernadette's life resumed its normal rhythm. She avoided going to the grotto because little girls were going there to play at seeing visions, and in any case on 15 June the municipal council forbade access to it and even put a fence round it. A war of barricades on a small scale broke out between the municipal workers and the good people of Lourdes. No sooner were the fences put up than they were torn down again two days later by unknown hands; no sooner were they put up again than they were again torn down, and so it went on: on 10 July they were put up for the fourth time.

But on 16 July, the feast of Our Lady of Mount Carmel, Bernadette felt the familiar call to go to the grotto. How could she obey her inner voice without disobeying authority? What she did was to stay on the right bank of the Gave, instead of crossing it by the Old Bridge, and thus reach the meadow where her faithful following always gathered to pray. Presently, in the half-light, Bernadette was on her knees reciting her rosary, and she entered into ecstasy. 'I didn't see the water, I didn't see the fence. I felt I was right at the grotto, no further away than all the other times. I saw nothing but the Blessed Virgin.' (BVP I: 162.) It was goodbye from Our Lady to her messenger, but it was also a prelude to those invisible visits that Bernadette would make from Nevers. She was always to remain attached to the grotto in spirit.

III   *The Message of Massabielle*

Massabielle, Gospel Territory

From among the eighteen appearances made by the Blessed Virgin to Bernadette, each of us will pick out what appeals to his temperament and spiritual climate, he will remember this word, that gesture, and these preferences are perfectly legitimate. But if we look at the event in the round, and with an eye to how it developed, we cannot fail to notice a resemblance between what happened at Massabielle and what the Gospels tell us of the life and mission of Jesus Christ. At the origin of everything, Light, a light that 'does not dazzle' but transfigures human existence; and, at the very heart of the world, the revelation of a Love that beatifies just by its presence, without words, by its beauty and goodness. From this foundation of light and love the message and the mission of prayer emerge, and, as in the Gospel, sin and sinners are there as anti-light and anti-love, as darkness turning away from light. It is the atmosphere of St John's Gospel that we breathe at Massabielle – the opposition between light and darkness; it is the atmosphere of St Paul's Epistles – the conflict between body and spirit; it is the atmosphere of the Apocalypse; in short, truth and life. And it was not just a happy chance that Aquerò finally revealed her name on 25 March, the feast of the Incarnation of the Word of God, or that the Name was identified with the mystery of Mary's Immaculate Conception, the mystery, pre-eminently, of pure love, of a humanity 'without spot, stain or wrinkle,' to use St Paul's words. In the destiny of the Virgin Mary, the mystery of the Immaculate Conception is the essential defeat of Satan and sin.

It is in this context that the Massabielle spring takes on its full significance. Water, especially in the marvel of its springs, plays a crucial part in the symbolism of the Bible: it gives life, or gives it again, it brings fertility, it cleanses, it refreshes, it heals. If Moses had not brought it forth from the rock in the desert, his whole people would have died of thirst; the psalms ceaselessly present God himself as 'the source of life', 'the source of salvation', 'the source of all joy', while in the Gospels, especially St John's, water is one of the main channels of Christ's beneficent action (cf. *John* 4, 5, 9,). Is not baptism the first sacrament? Baptism by penance and baptism in the Spirit at one and the same time, whence the believer emerges with 'new life'? When Bernadette scratched at the muddy puddle beneath the grotto at Massabielle and brought forth a little water, she obviously had no idea what this spring would mean to our world, but she lived it, she inserted herself through this experience into the very fabric of the history of salvation: by washing her face in that water mixed with earth, and by drinking it, she performed an act of penance; but once the water had regained the purity of its source, it would heal, it would refresh, it would sanctify.

Bernadette's first Communion on 3 June brought confirmation and fullness to the evangelical symbolism of the Spring, for the Eucharist is the sacrament about which we have to say with the psalmist: 'All our springs originate in you.' The fact that the whole Massabielle event should have had as its cause Bernadette's desire 'to make her first Communion' already evokes Our Lord's 'great desire' to fulfil his Passover. That her Communion should have taken place after the seventeenth appearance (rather as one appends a final stop to a text or a song) is not without its spiritual significance either: the Massabielle message was accomplished in the supreme act of Christ's love. But, it will be said, what relationship can there be between an event of ecclesiastical, world-wide importance and Bernadette's silent, intimate Communion? The rest of her life would provide the answer. Already on 3 June 1858 it was brought home to us that to live the message in the secrecy of the heart was more important than to tell it or bear witness to it in words – and this would become plainer still during the 'hidden life' at Nevers.

Throughout the eight years from 1858 until the morning of 4 July 1866 when she left Lourdes for Nevers, Bernadette repeated over and over again – whether to pilgrims or simply to the curious or sceptical – what she had 'seen and heard' at the grotto, and it is from this source that her biographers have collected their material. Yet in the eyes of God and Our Lady the true story of Lourdes had already been written: Bernadette and other souls with her were already living the message and offering themselves so that 'sinners' might be converted and brought into the love of God.

'The Best Proof of the Appearances – Bernadette' (Father Pomian). Her High Sense of Apostleship

Ever since the first appearance, Bernadette had been at pains to tell the whole truth and nothing but the truth concerning what she had 'heard and seen'. Never had any of her listeners been able to detect the slightest lie in what she said, nor the smallest addition or embellishment, nothing that savoured of a desire to draw attention to herself as a 'star'. Simplicity, fidelity, accuracy, restraint, detachment from self – these were the hallmarks of her accounts. This child, this girl, was in fact a woman with a highly developed conscience. Even her enemies, the unbelievers, were forced to pay homage to her integrity. 'For the Son of God, Jesus Christ.' said St Paul, 'was not Yes and No, but in him it is always Yes' (II *Corinthians* 1: 19), and Our Lord himself said to his apostles, according to St Matthew and St James, 'Let your yes be yes and your no be no'. An unswerving honesty is essential for every witness if he wants to be believed.

What is astonishing about Bernadette is that it was she herself who first demanded this honesty. At the 'familiarizing' appearance of 11 February she reacted against any possible self-deception. 'When I saw it (Aquerò) I rubbed my eyes, I thought I had made some mistake.' Then, as the vision continued to compel recognition, she clutched her rosary in her pocket as if for protection. After the vision had disappeared she checked with Toinette and Baloum as to whether they had experienced anything: 'I asked my companions whether they had seen anything. "No." they said . . . "Why, did you see anything?" "Oh no! If you didn't see anything, neither did I." . . . I was afraid I had been mistaken.' The following Saturday she went to consult Father Pomian in the confessional. And when she went to the grotto again on Sunday she armed herself with holy water so as to be able to test, as she thought, whether the Lady 'came from God'. Thus, though knowing nothing at all about supranormal mysticism, she spontaneously put into practice the doubt, the reserve, the resistance demanded by the spiritual masters.

This same balance and prudence shone forth in the course of Bernadette's cross-examinations by the civil and religious authorities. So long as the Lady herself had not disclosed her name, Bernadette refused to refer to her as the Virgin Mary. A short neuter dialect word allowed her to affirm the reality of what she had seen and heard without admit-

Right The old mill in Arcizac, where the Soubirous family lived in 1855

ting more than she had seen and heard: this word was Aquerò (it). 'And then you saw the Blessed Virgin?' asked Jacomet, the police inspector. 'I do not say that I saw the Blessed Virgin.' 'Well then, you didn't see anything.' 'Yes, I saw something.' 'Then what did you see?' 'Something white.' 'Something or someone?' 'Aquerò has the shape of a little girl.' 'And didn't Aquerò say: I am the Blessed Virgin?' 'Aquerò didn't say that.'

Bernadette displayed the same concern for accuracy when she had to appear before the ecclesiastical judges who had been instructed to conduct an inquiry into the events at Massabielle. The bishops' statement of 18 January 1862 made this very plain. It would seem that what had convinced these learned and punctilious men was the visionary's 'sincerity,' 'simplicity,' candour,' and 'modesty'. 'Always in agreement with herself, she has, in the various interrogations to which she has been submitted, consistently maintained what she has already said, adding nothing to it, taking nothing from it.' and the statement stressed 'the wisdom of her answers', her 'upright spirit', her 'calm imagination', her 'common sense above her age'. In short she appears to have displayed all the qualities of the human conscience recommended by St Paul to Christians living in a pagan society: 'Whatever is true, whatever is honourable, whatever is just, whatever is pure . . . think about these things.' (*Phil.* 4: 8.)

The words evocative of Joan of Arc, or rather of the Curé d'Ars, said by Bernadette in the course of conversations with pilgrims and tourists are quoted everywhere. Like all 'historic' utterances they have been somewhat touched up, but many have an authentic ring. On 28 August 1858 she said to Father Fonteneau, the future Bishop of Agen, who did not believe in the appearances: 'I'm not forcing you to believe me, I can only tell you what I saw and heard.' To other unbelievers she said: 'I have been told to tell you about it, I have not been told to make you believe it.'

The Count of Bruissard, a 'hardened sinner' by his own admission, did not believe in the appearances, yet he was 'struck' by Bernadette's 'simplicity and conviction'. 'Well now', he said to her, 'how did the Lady smile?' 'Oh sir, you would have to come from heaven to reproduce that smile.' 'Couldn't you reproduce it for me? I am a sceptic and don't believe in visions.' 'As you are a sinner', replied Bernadette, 'I shall reproduce the Blessed Virgin's smile for you.'

At the end of 1859 a Protestant magistrate and legal expert talked with Bernadette. At the end of their conversation he declared to Father Boyer: 'In my view the strength of conviction is there. This child amazes me and moves me. There is certainly something there.'

Left The altar in the choir of the parish church of Bartrès

That 'something' was felt by many people. People who arrived as sceptics and went away convinced – even ecclesiastics, even bishops. Bernadette's objectivity was overwhelming, irresistible. At Nevers it was the same as at Lourdes.

After the bishops' statement of 1862 someone set a trap for Bernadette. Everything is summed up in her reply which would be too clever were it not so artless. 'And if the Bishop of Tarbes had come to the conclusion that you were mistaken, what would you have said?' 'I would never have been able to say that I didn't see or hear.'

But over the purity of Bernadette's evidence there hung another danger which came from outside. The more she won over hearts and souls to the cause of the appearances, the more was she the focus of attention, not to say veneration, and the more she risked having money showered upon her, for this is the way the world shows its admiration. Threats closed in from all sides and from the most unexpected quarters. Everyone wanted to see her, touch her, hear her, snatch a 'relic' from her. If she took part in any ceremony people tried to cut off a piece of her hood, her veil, her dress. 'How stupid you are!' she said to these fanatics, but to no purpose. Her rosary particularly aroused cupidity. An archbishop proposed that she should exchange it for his rosary mounted in gold; she refused. Then one day she 'lost' it in circumstances redolent of pious pilfering. People asked her for medals, pictures, 'portraits' (the word for early photographs) and every kind of absurd souvenir, even hair! To Madame Douville of Saint-Alyre, who asked for this souvenir, she wrote on 24 February 1865: 'As for hair, I am expressly forbidden to give it away; had there been anything else that I could have given you without disobedience I would have done so with all my heart!' Which tells a long tale!

Where autographs (already!) were concerned, the difficulty was to escape both from vanity and the importunity of admirers. She signed her name but preceded it with p.p., signifying 'Pray for (*priez pour*) Bernadette'. As she did not write very well she practised the above formula in a rough note book, and one day wrote 'Pray Bernadette', a choice item for the 'devil's advocate' in her canonisation trial, but luckily he did not notice this advance self-canonisation!

How was it that all this adulation did not turn Bernadette's head? In fact the reverse was the case. She complained of it and tried to avoid it whenever she possibly could. She said it 'tired' her. A strange star indeed!

But there was a more serious matter. Whether orally or by letter, she was beset by requests for prayers, prayers for special intentions, for the sick, for needs of various kinds. Bernadette considered it a duty to answer; she did not evade the issue; she promised, but always on one condition, that her correspondents would, in turn, pray for 'poor Bernadette'. As long as she lived at Lourdes she took delight in fulfilling her promise, 'especially when I have the joy of going to the grotto'. After she went to Nevers she told her Lourdes correspondents to pray for her 'especially when you go to the grotto'.

A collection could be made of Bernadette's *fioretti*, flowers not manufactured but culled from her life itself, her correspondence itself. And they would be much more enchanting than legendary flowers!

Bernadette's Life from 1858 to 1866

We shall briefly indicate the main events of these eight years.

After the Appearances, Bernadette continued to live with her family in the former prison. She attended the free school, the school for the poor, and at fourteen years old gave the impression of a 'backward pupil' among the little girls learning to read and write. Her mother often needed her at home, which had not helped her studies. And now there were all those visitors among whom were illustrious personages against whom the door could not be shut: Admiral Bruat's wife, the Prince Imperial's governess, Louis Veuillot, to mention but a few. And then there were bishops.

In September the Soubirous left the prison cell for lodgings that were hardly bigger but more salubrious: a room in the house of Deluc, the pastry-cook.

Some time during the first three months of 1859 there was yet another move: François wanted to try his luck again as a miller at the mill at Gras. At this time Bernadette was sent to Cauterets, so as to rescue her from all the visits that tired her and to nurse her asthma. But as soon as she returned to Lourdes, everything started up again.

In July 1860 extreme measures had to be taken. Through a shrewd decision on the part of the mayor, Lacadé, Bernadette was admitted to the municipal hospice run by the Sisters of Nevers. She was admitted as a penniless invalid, but she was to attend the classes of the 'paying school' for well-to-do girls. It was hard to leave the poor, and attending the classes was not much more than a formality. From time to time she 'went down' to the grotto or the mill, always escorted by a sister for protection. At this time there began the ordeal of photographers: Father Bernadou to begin with, and then Billard-Perrin, Dufour, Viron and

Prouvost; they were to follow her as far as Nevers! These 'portraits' were sold for a few pence to help with the financing of the sanctuaries. 'It's all I am worth', was Bernadette's comment.

The first of Bernadette's letters to be preserved date from 1861, the most important among them, perhaps, being the account of the appearances that Father Gondrand asked her to write. They are humble documents in which – as in all her writings – the contents that were genuinely her own had to be sifted from borrowed phrases and corrections put in by others. But such as they are they are irreplaceable.

On 18 January 1862 there appeared the official statement issued by Monsignor Laurence, Bishop of Tarbes, in which the events at Massabielle were given episcopal authentication. At the end of March Bernadette fell seriously ill – we do not know whether she was suffering from pneumonia or an acute attack of her asthma – but she recovered after being given Extreme Unction on 28 April. Nevertheless during the years 1862–6 she was away from Lourdes several times on account of her health.

When in Lourdes she continued to board at the hospice of the Sisters of Nevers. It was there that she was interviewed by the celebrated sculptor, Fabisch, who had been commissioned by some nuns near Lyon to create the statue of the Virgin of the Appearances. The finished work did not altogether satisfy our visionary. It was inaugurated on 4 April 1864, but neither Bernadette nor Father Peyramale was able to be present at the ceremony.

Bernadette's Vocation

Meanwhile a serious question was occupying Bernadette's mind and heart: her vocation.

It might have been thought that she would enter the order of the Sisters of Nevers as a matter of course. Surely a girl who had seen the· Blessed Virgin would become a nun, and surely she would seek admission with the sisters who had taken her in to their hospice, looked after her and educated her?

In fact things were not so straightforward as that. Dom Bernard Billet has patiently unravelled the threads of this complicated story (SA, Vol.

Right Bernadette sees the White Lady. Chalk drawing by an unknown artist in the Bernadette Museum in the Convent of Saint Gildard in Nevers. The drawing carries a dedication to the 'Countess of Geoffre' and the 'Count of Nouy'

ERNADETTE·DE·LOURDES·

Bernadette at prayer. A photo taken in the Dufour workshop in Tarbes

Left A statue of Mary by the sculptor Fabisch which was placed in the Grotto of Massabielle in 1864

The cloister in the Hospice of the Sisters of Nevers in Lourdes, where Bernadette lived and worked during 1860 – 66

Bernadette with Mother Alexandrine Roques, Superior of the Hospice at Lourdes

The bridge at Betharram over which Bernadette crossed many times in order to seek advice from Michel Garicoïts, who was later canonized

The Lacadé mill in Lourdes, in which Bernadette's parents lived from 1863. The remaining part of this building is pointed out in Lourdes as the parental home of Bernadette, although in fact during this time she was living in the Hospice. Her father, François Soubirous, is sitting on the bench

A room in the Lacadé mill in Lourdes, the home of Bernadette's family

Bernadette with other girls from the Hospice at Lourdes. A photo taken on the occasion of her departure for Nevers

A photo of Bernadette taken in 1866 seated amongst her maternal relations

Mother Marie-Thérèse Vauzou, Bernadette's novice mistress and later Mother Superior of the congregation of the Sisters of Nevers.

Mother Joséphine Imbert, Mother Superior at the time of Bernadette's novitiate at Nevers

Father Jean-Baptiste de Laveyne, founder of the congregation of the Sisters of Nevers

Right The source in the Grotto of Massabielle today

VIII) and I shall try to summarize his most important conclusions, with the addition of a few details suggested by the correspondence (ESB, 218 et seq.).

That Bernadette chose her 'state of life' freely and of her own accord is made amply plain in these documents. Her vocation had nothing to do with the three personal secrets confided to her by the Lady of Massabielle.

Another established fact: her desire to 'become a nun' antedated by some years her decision to enter with the Sisters of Nevers (whose full name is the Sisters of Charity and Christian Instruction).

What was the date of her decision to become a nun? We are not sure. The letter of 9 April 1858, in which Adelaide Monlaur reports a conversation between 'several gentlemen, including the mayor of Lourdes, and Bernadette', presents many problems. Adelaide Monlaur is not considered a reliable witness on the whole, and how, through whom, had she acquired the information that she reports? The import of what she says, however, is probable: thus Bernadette would have wanted to become a nun ever since the time of the appearances.

Nor can Aunt Bernarde's assertion, that Bernadette had first considered entering Carmel, be regarded as reliable.

On the other hand it seems certain that towards 1860–1 Bernadette seriously envisaged joining the 'Saint-Bernard' nuns, an order founded by Father Costac at Anglet, near Bayonne, which was attracting many girls of the region. She had certainly heard talk of the life of penance and prayer led by these nuns, and it is said that she even sought admission to the novitiate. Apparently it was the founder himself who refused her request. No doubt he remembered the attempts made by Mélanie, the visionary of La Salette, to enter the religious life. 'I don't want crowds pouring to Notre-Dame to get a glimpse of her', he said.

Bernadette's attraction towards the hidden, silent, mortified life of the 'Saint-Bernard' nuns gives us our first insight into the underlying motives of her religious vocation. It was a vocation that coincided with her mission received at Massabielle. Especially as at Anglet Father Costac admitted some of the 'penitents' from the Refuge of which he was in charge. A feeling for silence, prayer and mortification was never absent from the letters Bernadette later wrote to men and women who had entered the religious life.

However this may be, here we see Bernadette coming up against one of the obstacles to being admitted into a religious order: her fame as a messenger!

Left With this umbrella and bag Bernadette stood before the door of the Convent of Saint Gildard in Nevers on 7 July 1866. She was received here as a novice under the name of Marie-Bernard on 29 July

Between 1861 and 1863 the achievement of her desire to be a nun seemed to recede yet further. Her health deteriorated. On 28 April 1862 she was thought to be dying. So her poor health was the second obstacle to her vocation. The third obstacle was her lack of education, and as she realized this she tried hard to make good the deficiency. A fourth obstacle, at least where certain orders were concerned, was her lack of dowry. She was a 'pauper'.

However, a serene state of soul took possession of her at this time. She would wait for a sign that would show her God's will.

And in 1863 a light broke through the darkness. At this time she was helping in the hospice infirmary where she was entrusted with the care of 'rather disgusting' old people. 'She applied herself to the work with love. She came to like it.' So she succeeded. She wasn't so 'incompetent' and 'good for nothing' as all that! What was her tally? She was excellent at needlework and embroidery, good at looking after little girls, and a skilful nurse of old people, her care of whom no-one challenged – that was quite a lot to make her useful in this large establishment. So why was she not satisfied with this humble, simple existence? Especially as her life looked as if it was going to be short. What was the use of forming new projects? 'I am waiting', she said to anyone who asked her about the future. Round about this period she wrote to Sister Vincent Garros: 'I like nursing the sick. I was given one to look after when I was well' – it was a drunken old woman who had fallen head first into the fire – 'No-one pays any attention to me. I shall stay here.'

On 27 September 1863 Monsignor Forcade, Bishop of Nevers, came to Lourdes. He asked to have a private interview with Bernadette.

The interview started with Bernadette giving an account of the appearances, and the bishop noted that she expressed herself 'without searching for words . . . She is imperturbable and nothing upsets her.' In other words he, like other visitors, had tried to catch her out.

Then, without further ado, the bishop propounded his plan.

'And now, my child, what are you going to be?'

'Nothing.'

'What do you mean, nothing? You have to be something in this poor world.'

'Very well. I am with the Sisters.'

'No doubt, but you're only here on a temporary basis.'

'I would happily stay for ever.'

Bernadette, with her brief answers, showed herself more than able to demolish the most skilfully prepared assaults. She had been with the Sisters for three years; why should this happy balance between work and mission not continue? As an idea it was not outlandish.

Monsignor Forcade renewed the attack. 'That's easy to say, but not so easy to bring about. The fact that you've been taken in provisionarily and out of charity does not mean that you can be kept here for ever.' Monsignor was moving onto shifting sands. Bernadette regained the advantage with a sharp:

'Why not?'

And Monsignor plunged deeper into an argument which he knew was worthless: 'Because you are not a Sister, and as you know it is necessary to be a Sister if you want to be admitted into the community on a permanent basis. You aren't even a servant here. You are, at this moment, exactly what you claimed to be: you are nothing. And no-one lasts long anywhere on that footing.'

Then he changed his tactics and decided to refer to 'settling down' in the sense of working at home and marriage.

'Oh no, certainly not that!' answered Bernadette with spirit.

Now Monsignor was able to get back to his project. 'Then why don't you become a Sister? A Sister at Nevers? Haven't you ever thought of that?'

And again Bernadette's answer fell like a chopper: 'That's impossible. You know how poor I am. I would never have the necessary dowry.' (Forcade, p. 11–12.)

With a word Monsignor reassured her on this score: 'Once we recognize a true vocation in penniless girls, we don't hesitate to receive them without a dowry.'

Then Bernadette put forward her second objection which had been worrying her for some time: 'But the girls that you take in without a dowry are skilled or clever and make good your losses. But as for me, I am nothing. I am good for nothing.'

Now it was for Monsignor to play his trump card. 'But this morning I noticed that you are very good at something.'

'At what?'

'At scraping carrots. You will always be able to do that and it is badly needed at the Mother House. And then we have nurses at Nevers. There would be no difficulty in finding ways of using you, and during your novitiate we would not fail to give you some of the education that you never had.'

'If that is how it is, Monsignor, I shall think about it, but I haven't made up my mind yet.'

In the event of Bernadette deciding to become a nun at Nevers, Monsignor Forcade took it on himself 'to look after the rest'. It was in fact less easy than he had anticipated: Mother Superior Imbert and her advisers at Nevers had no wish to take in a famous visionary who, moreover, already seemed to be a 'pillar of the infirmary'. However by the end of the year they had succumbed to Monsignor Forcade's pressure. But Bernadette on her side still felt 'no attraction'.

'I shall think about . . .' How long did this thinking period last? The excellent biographers, Father Laurentin and Dom Bernard Billet, fix the date of Bernadette's decision as 4 April 1864. They base this date on the evidence of Sister Maria Géraud:

'After Mass at which she had received Holy Communion, Bernadette managed to draw the Superior (Mother Alexandrine Roques) to one side. "I now know, my dear Mother, where I must enter." "Where, my child?" "With you, my dear Mother!" "Very well, we'll talk about it with Monsignor."' (DA, VIII, p. 109, and the long note on the 'decision' of 4 April.) And the biographer adds: 'Sister Maria Géraud was convinced that it was in the Communion she had just received that Bernadette found the light that decided her on her religious vocation.'

Is the evidence from Sister Maria Géraud – who was merely passing through Lourdes to attend the inauguration of Fabisch's statue – sufficiently reliable for an accurate dating of such an important event? Bernadette's own correspondence gives a more complicated picture of the path that led to her decision.

Writing on 2 May 1864 to Mother Ursule Fardes (Superior of the hospice at the time of the appearances, and one of her confidants), Bernadette makes no mention of her decision. But this silence could be explained by the fact that she was going through another bout of ill-health at the time and was envisaging an early death rather than entering a convent! (ESB, 155.)

Another clue is provided by Bernadette's letter of 22 August 1864 to Father Bouin who had confided to her his intention of 'becoming a hermit at Massabielle'. Returning confidence for confidence, Bernadette confessed to him: 'I would very much like to be able to do the same as you, for I am weary of seeing so many people; pray for me, I beg you, either that God will take me or that He will soon let me become one of His brides, for that is my deepest desire, unworthy as I am.' (ESB, 162.) This letter confirms Bernadette's desire to become a nun but makes no mention of her having chosen the Sisters of Nevers.

In the present state of our archives, we have to wait until 4 December 1865 for a clear indication of the fact, but not the date, of her decision: 'I would very much like my health to improve,' she wrote to Mother Augustine Ceyrac; 'I would be so happy to belong to the family of the Sisters of Nevers.' (ESB, 173.)

Right A view which looks over the 15-arched Loire bridge towards the Cathedral of Nevers

But now the matter becomes more complicated. To this same Mother Ceyrac she wrote on 28 April 1866: 'I am feeling more eager than ever to leave the world, and now that I have definitely made up my mind, I propose to enter very soon.' (ESB, 183.) And on the following 15 June she wrote to Mother Ursule Fardes (to whom she had not mentioned her vocation in her letter of 2 May 1864): 'Knowing how interested you are in me, I am happy to tell you that I have at last decided to enter your Order.' (ESB, 190.) And she reminded Mother Fardes, who had left Lourdes in 1861, of this charming incident: 'I think of you often, my dear Mother, and I like to remember the day when we were in the woodshed and you talked to me about my vocation. How often have I remembered that little conversation! I feel I can still see you sitting on one step, and myself on the other; I look at them whenever I go there.'

Given this network of confidences complicated by silences, perhaps we should abandon the idea of fixing the date when Bernadette 'finally decided to enter' the order of the Sisters of Nevers. Only one thing is certain, that her request for admission to the novitiate was sent off shortly before 28 April 1866. A letter from Mother Alexandrine Roques to Mother Ceyrac (1 May 1866) assures us that: '[Bernadette] has already started to take [your pills], happy to think that she will thus be strong enough to go to Nevers; that is her sole desire which she has just communicated to the novice mistress who has already answered, reassuring her as to all her fears.' (ESB, 184.) Unfortunately neither Bernadette's letter nor Mother Vauzou's reply has ever been traced.

Matters may well have developed as follows: In September 1863, the interview with Monsignor Forcade; then a time of reflection at some point during which Bernadette felt drawn to the Sisters of Nevers, an inclination she confided to Mother Alexandrine Roques; then a period of ill-health throwing everything into jeopardy; then emergence from this health crisis and in 1866 the decision to enter the order of the Sisters of Nevers; finally, at the end of April, the request for admission while expressing 'all her fears'. What a pity that we do not know what these 'fears' were; they would perhaps provide the key to the problem! The above is only a hypothesis, but it has the advantage of staying within the known texts.

The progress of Bernadette's religious vocation in fact remains very obscure to us. The only people who could have provided information on the subject were Father Pomian from whom she had always sought and found advice and help, and the saintly Michel Garicoïts whom she

Left The Church of the Convent of Saint Gildard in Nevers, in which as a novice Bernadette entered the Congregation of the 'Sisters of Charity and of Christian Instruction of Nevers' under the name 'Sister Marie-Bernard'

consulted on several occasions at Betharram, and to whom she went to confession, but who died on Thursday, 14 May 1863 (even before the interview with Monsignor Forcade). It has been suggested that Bernadette kept a notebook about her vocation. Father Cros moved heaven and earth to trace it, but in vain. Perhaps the most valuable evidence is the letter written to her by the famous Father Alix when she left Lourdes, a letter she took with her to Nevers and transcribed in 1873 or 1874. (ESB, 386.) This letter, which incidentally corresponded at a deep level to the guidance Father Pomian and Father Peyramale had given her, revealed to Bernadette what she already recognized: namely, that over and above any vocation to the religious life, she had a personal vocation, that of living the message of Massabielle in all its rigour. And the marvel was that the spirituality instilled into the Sisters of Nevers by Father de Laveyne was in full harmony with the message of Massabielle.

Be this as it may, we know from Mother Alexandrine Roques' letter, quoted above, that by 1 May 1866 Bernadette had been reassured and admitted to the novitiate of the Convent of Saint-Gildard at Nevers. What had happened between 1864 and April 1866? As we outlined above, crises of health alternating with periods of remission, a stay at Momères with her cousin Jeanne Vedère (4 October–19 November 1864), visits to the communities at Pau and Oloron. On receiving Mother Vauzou's letter at the end of April 1866, she became a postulant and as such was integrated into the community of the hospice sisters where she stayed for the first three months of her novitiate. Sometimes she helped the sister in the infirmary to tend the sick, sometimes she looked after the children in the school, and meanwhile she continued with her own education. This was a perfectly regular situation, many postulants prepared themselves in this way. The date of the departure for Nevers depended on the Bishop of Tarbes – he might want her to stay on a little longer at Lourdes 'for the good of the grotto'. (ESB, 184.) The fact was that he was already planning the inauguration of the Crypt and he wanted Bernadette to be there – her presence would attract visitors and alms! But there was the reverse side of the coin. At the big procession on 19 May Bernadette was dressed in the anonymous uniform of the Children of Mary and concealed behind a white veil; but in vain! – the crowd identified her and indulged in the usual excesses. Everyone wanted to see her, touch her, cut bits from her veil. On the following two days pilgrims thronged to the hospice and asked for Bernadette. She was made to walk for a while in the cloister, flanked by two nuns. Bernadette didn't like it at all. 'Oh Mother, you show me off like a fatted ox . . . You show me off like some strange animal,' she groaned.

The departure was finally fixed for early in July. Meanwhile, on 26

May, Bernadette had persuaded Léontine Mouret's father to let his daughter go to Nevers too, and her letter had the desired effect; they were to do the journey together. (ESB, 188 and ANDL 42, 1910, p. 3.) Then came the time for farewells. On 2 July the photographer, Viron, obtained permission from the Bishop of Tarbes to take souvenir photographs: Bernadette alone, Bernadette with her family, Bernadette with other Lourdes girls, Bernadette with sisters from the hospice, even Bernadette clothed as a professed nun, thereby anticipating canon law, but this piece of audacity has enabled us to have an interesting picture of the future Sister Marie-Bernard before the rather conventional poses of the photographs taken later at Nevers.

Visits and leave-taking continued throughout the day of 3 July. That evening there was a family meal in the kitchen of the mill, Moulin Lacadé; a gathering of intimates round the girl who was going away. But before that Bernadette paid her last visit to the grotto.

Bernadette's Undying Goodbye to the Grotto

On her last pilgrimage to the grotto, Bernadette would certainly have been accompanied by a few intimate friends, if only to 'protect' her from unwanted admirers; but unfortunately none of these witnesses has left an account of the event, so biographers have had to delve into their imaginations to make good the gap. Did Bernadette say on this occasion, 'Leave me for a moment more', or the famous, 'The Grotto was my heaven'? It is plausible but not certain. Another track open to our investigation is Bernadette's heart. What did the Grotto of Massabielle mean to Bernadette?

Bernadette's own accounts of the appearances provide an answer to this question: the grotto was the high place of her soul, the setting for a marvellous and unique experience; it was 'heaven'. And the grotto was also the context of her 'mission', a mission extending far beyond place and events, a mission of the Church, a mission on a world scale. The grotto was also the setting for her personal sacrifice, for demands were made there as much as joy bestowed. In short, was not the grotto for Bernadette in some way similar to what stones were for Abraham, Moses and other great 'visionaries' of the Bible – those stones with which they set up an 'altar' as a sign of adoration, of thanksgiving, of sacrifice, of perpetual commitment? As the witness to a covenant?

On this point the correspondence is eloquent. In December 1862, that is to say in one of her very first letters, Bernadette wrote to Don Antonio Morales: 'You ask for a variety of objects, but all I can send you, to my regret, is a medal of the blessed Grotto; that is all I possess at the moment.' (ESB, 150.) Ever since she had lived at the hospice, that is to say since 1860, she had never been able to go to the grotto except accompanied by one or two sisters to protect her against the inquisitiveness of pilgrims. Whenever she went there in that way it was 'a joy'. 'I think of you often,' she wrote, for instance, to the nuns of Lacour in May 1864, 'especially when I have the joy of going to the Grotto. It is there that I pray for all your intentions.' It was there that she discharged her debts of gratitude and responded to the demands of friendship. 'I do assure you,' she wrote at the end of 1865 to M. Duvroux, 'that I seldom pass a day without thinking of you all, and especially if I have the joy of going to the Grotto, it is there that I like to remember my friends, at the feet of my good Mother.' (ESB, 176.) And to Mother Ursule Fardes (15 June 1866): 'I think of you whenever I have the joy of going to the Grotto; it is there that I pray to my good Mother to grant you all the graces that you need. I had a private intention for you on the day I had the joy of attending the holy sacrifice of the Mass and receiving Holy Communion for the first time in the church hewn out of the ground over the Grotto.' Suffice it to say that the grotto was much more than a beautiful memory for Bernadette, it was the setting for her personal and apostolic prayer.

Once she was at Nevers, things were the other way round. When writing to correspondents in Lourdes she asked them to pray for her, especially when they went to the grotto. Hardly had she arrived at the novitiate than she wrote to the sisters at the hospice (20 July): 'I beg you to be so good as to offer a few prayers for this intention of mine' —it was a thanksgiving—'and especially when you go to the Grotto. That is where you will find me in spirit, close to the foot of the rock that I love so much.' (ESB, 242.) And this formula often recurs in her letters. So what was it that she loved so much at the grotto? It was what lay beyond the grotto, it was the call to prayer and sacrifice that she heard there. When the then Bishop of Nevers, Monsignor Ladoue, was leaving for Lourdes at the end of June 1876, he asked her if she would like to accompany the pilgrims, and she replied: 'Oh no, Monsignor, I would prefer to stay in my bed' (her sick bed). The fulfilment of the mission which she had received at the grotto meant more to her than seeing the grotto again. Her utterances concerning the grotto were innumerable. One of the most remarkable was reported by Sister Marcelline Lanessan, when she, too, had asked Bernadette if she would like to go back to Lourdes. 'Oh no,' she replied, 'people would leave the Blessed Virgin and follow me. But pray for me at the Grotto.' She was always anxious to efface herself before the Blessed Virgin, just as the Blessed Virgin was always anxious to stand aside for her Son.

Bernadette's love for the rock at Massabielle has echoes in the Bible. In the Bible the Rock is the symbol for God, for his steadfastness, his presence, his fidelity, his eternity. 'There is no Rock like our God . . .'; 'Come shout with joy for our God, let us acclaim our Rock, our Salvation!' And when Christ wanted to found his Church, 'against which the powers of hell would not prevail', he changed the name of Simon into Peter, meaning Rock.

From Lourdes to Nevers

Early in the morning of 4 July 1866, Bernadette crossed the short space separating the hospice from the station of Lourdes. Her close relations and a few friends accompanied her. She was carrying an umbrella and a large canvas bag. There were the final embraces. Then Bernadette left Lourdes, never to return. The railway line ran along beside the River Gave and passed opposite Massabielle. Bernadette looked at the grotto for the last time. Her mission was continuing . . .

Bernadette has left us a description of this journey in a letter she wrote from Nevers to the sisters of the hospice. She also gives us her impressions of her first days at the Saint-Gildard Convent.

'Now let me tell you about the journey and how we did it. We arrived at Bordeaux at six o'clock on Wednesday evening and stayed there till one o'clock on Friday. I do assure you that we took full advantage of the time to go around, and by carriage if you please! We visited all the houses. I have the honour of telling you that they aren't at all like our house at Lourdes, and especially the imperial seminary; it looks more like a palace than a religious house. We went to see the Carmelites' church and from there we went to the Garonne to see the ships. And then we went to the zoo; and there we saw something quite new: guess what? fish: red, black, white, grey; that's what I found best of all, seeing those little creatures swimming about in front of a crowd of kids who stood staring at them.

'We spent that night at Périgueux. The next morning we set off at seven o'clock and arrived at Nevers towards half past ten in the evening.'

At that late hour the Saint-Gildard Convent was asleep, or pretending to be asleep: just a few nuns were still awake to take the new arrivals to their dormitory.

It was understood that the next day Bernadette would relate the story of the appearances to all the communities of Nevers who would assemble at Saint-Gildard for the purpose, and that thereafter the event would be shrouded in silence: the postulant would never talk about it again nor would any sister question her. This regulation was a wise one and Bernadette was in full agreement with her superiors: 'I have come here to hide', as she often said. She had been longing for the anonymity and silence of community life. The very first letters of hers that we possess show how tired she was of being the centre: 'I am weary of seeing so many people.' (ESB, 182.) She hoped that once she was at Nevers her role as a star would end for ever.

That first Sunday, 8 July, was not passed without the shedding of tears. 'I have to tell you', wrote Bernadette to the Sisters at the hospice, 'that Léontine [Mouret] and I watered Sunday with our tears!' But Bernadette was not one to indulge her sorrows. 'I do assure you that the sacrifice would be much more bitter if we had to leave our dear novitiate! One feels that this is the house of God, one has to love it in spite of oneself!' (ESB, 241.) When, during these early days, her heart was too full to bear, she went to 'cry it out in front of Our Lady of the Waters at the far end of the garden'. To her this statue of the Virgin in some way resembled the Lady of Massabielle – which seems strange to us today.

So Lourdes was not forgotten and never would be. Nevers was a continuation of Lourdes, a fulfilment of Lourdes. In 1858 the message of Massabielle had made Bernadette enter more deeply into the mystery of her baptism; now, her consecration in the religious life made her enter more deeply into the message of Massabielle. An astonishing continuity was to mark her life. At Nevers she was both fully the daughter of Father de Laveyne and fully faithful to the message of Massabielle. There was never any perceptible tension between her vocation to the Order and her personal vocation: the two vocations blended: and this alone was a proof of the deep level at which the two calls sounded within her.

Sister Philomène Tourré, whose task it was to initiate the young postulant into the ways of the novitiate, has left us the following little story: 'One day when we were in the courtyard together, Bernadette showed me three small stones. "These are my companions whom I love", she said. On one of them she had written "Lourdes", on the second "the Grotto", and on the third "Nevers, Mother-House". 'It amuses me, diverts me, and brings back many memories.'' (ESB, 246.)

IV *Bernadette's Religious Life*

For thirteen years, from July 1866 to April 1879, Bernadette's home was this imposing Convent of Saint-Gildard. She was more often inside the house than outside, more often in the infirmaries than in the community rooms. It was a life whose prayerful monotony unfolded to the rhythm not only of its canonical stages but also of the fluctuations in her health. The events that took place in the world, except for those concerned with the Church and especially Rome and the Pope, passed unnoticed in Bernadette's religious life. But beneath this quiet sameness of her days, and quiet sameness of her tasks, there burned a fiery flame of love for Jesus Christ, for the Church and for sinners. It is a marvellous and simple story, and with the help of the few clues and pointers that have come down to us we shall try to reconstruct it.

The Outer Life

On 29 July 1866 Bernadette received the religious habit together with 43 other postulants. Thereafter she was known as Sister Marie-Bernard.

A fortnight later, round about 14 August, she entered the infirmary, though without being completely out of action: indeed it was now that she inaugurated her service as assistant-nurse which was her most constant occupation at Saint-Gildard. But soon her condition worsened. Towards the beginning of September she was confined to her bed, and on 25 October she received Extreme Unction for the second time in her short life. In accordance with canon law, Monsignor Forcade authorized that her religious profession should be put forward. He came to Saint-Gildard to receive it, but as Sister Marie-Bernard was too weak to say the words herself, he said them for her, and the invalid answered: 'Amen'.

In February 1867 Sister Marie-Bernard was able to resume to a certain extent the life of the novitiate. Though her health was still frail, she was able to make her regular profession on 30 October together with her 43 companions. It was a temporary profession and would, according to the Constitutions of the Sisters of Nevers, be freely renewed every year. On the evening of the ceremony, the newly-professed nuns received their 'obedience' from the bishop and the Mother Superior, that is to say their 'employment' in one or other of the houses of the Order. The Mother Superior decided to keep Sister Marie-Bernard here at Saint-Gildard. As this was considered to be a privilege, a scenario was planned with Monsignor Forcade to ensure that Sister Marie-Bernard would not draw any pride from this decision. Much has been made of the following episode recounted by Monsignor Forcade himself. But in order to understand it properly we must imagine the look on the faces, the smiles, the whole atmosphere of the assembly. The Mother General said to the bishop:

'Monsignor, she is good for nothing . . . But if you wish it we could keep her here at the Mother House out of charity and employ her in some way in the infirmary, perhaps to do the cleaning and prepare the infusions.'

Monsignor Forcade then asked Bernadette: 'Is it true, Sister Marie-Bernard, that you are good for nothing?'

To which Bernadette replied: 'I told you that myself, at Lourdes, when you were trying to persuade me to enter the community, and you said it didn't matter.'

And this took place in front of the whole General Council!

From 1867 to 3 June the community diary tells of frequent periods of ill-health for Sister Marie-Bernard. On 26 March 1870 Mother Superior Imbert left for Rome to present the Constitutions of the Order and have them approved. She returned on 7 July. This was the period of the First Vatican Council and everyone was aware of its importance. The political situation in both Italy and France was stormy. In Italy the establishment of national unity was threatening the integrity of the Papal States and the Pope's independence. In France war broke out with Germany. In August the Mother Superior put the Sisters of Nevers at the service of the War Ministry to nurse the wounded. On 3 October Saint-Gildard was turned into a hospital. Between 16 and 20 December the sisters 'took various measures in case they had to pack their bags and move'. The 25th of December was a bleak Christmas at Saint-Gildard, no midnight Mass, no office.

On 20 April 1870 Bernadette had taken over responsibility for the infirmary as the head nurse was seriously ill. But Bernadette herself suffered various spells of illness and in January 1873 was again confined to her bed. On 3 June she received Extreme Unction for the third time.

In early January 1874 Sister Marie-Bernard, whose health had somewhat improved, was appointed assistant-sacristan. But even this modest

Right This statue of 'Our Dear Lady of the Waters' at the end of the convent garden of Saint Gildard, was especially loved by Bernadette as it reminded her of the Grotto at Lourdes

employment proved too arduous for her. In April 1875 she was again in bed and from this time she became a perpetual invalid.

In September 1878 she was able to go downstairs for the second-to-last time – to the chapel for a ceremony which brought her 'deep joy'. She made her perpetual vows in accordance with the new Constitutions – her health had prevented her from making them at the same time the year before with the companions with whom she had made her first profession. And being for this reason the most senior of the professed nuns it was she who read the formal words in the name of all the sisters. She looked on her perpetual profession as 'a great grace'.

Gradually Sister Marie-Bernard's health deteriorated. On 28 March 1879 she again received Extreme Unction. On the evening of 15 April her condition became critical. On 16 April, shortly before three o'clock in the afternoon, Sister Marie-Bernard entered into the joy of her Lord.

Such was the external framework of Bernadette's life at Nevers. We will not say 'the events' of her life, so insignificant was it to the human eye, and so ceaselessly threatened by illness. But beneath the insignificance God was secretly working and drawing the chosen one of the Lady of Massabielle up to the purest heights of union with Jesus Christ: in her was fulfilled all that was most intense, and at the same time most 'simple', in Our Lord's discourse after the Last Supper as recorded by St John.

The Inner Life

It is God's work in Sister Marie-Bernard's inner life that we shall now attempt to trace, and we shall do so under the headings suggested by the chaplain of Saint-Gildard, Father Febvre. According to him, she 'lived out' the teachings given her by the Virgin at Massabielle – to do penance, to pray, to suffer for sinners – on three levels, (1) through the physical suffering which hardly ever left her, (2) through moral suffering, (3) through spiritual suffering; so it is these that we shall now consider.

Her physical sufferings
As we have already seen, Bernadette's years as a nun were accompanied by the slow and implacable destruction of her 'poor body', her 'earthly

Left In the choir of the convent church of Saint Gildard stands, since her beatification on 14 June 1925, the shrine containing the body of Bernadette, who on 8 December 1933, on the Feast of the Immaculate Conception, was received into the ranks of the saints

garment', to use St Paul's language. After her death, the Mother Superior told Father Cros: 'She suffered a great deal; she spent more time in the infirmary than anywhere else. During her last months it sometimes took her an hour to find a bearable position, during which time her face altogether changed, she became as if dead. She who encountered suffering with such courage was defeated by her pain . . . Even when asleep, the faintest movement of her leg made her cry out . . . She passed whole nights without sleeping. During the winter before her death there were such sharp cries that her companions in the dormitory could not sleep. She became smaller in her sufferings, she shrank to nothing'. (ESB, 516.) Yet Sister Marie-Bernard never mentioned her suffering in her letters, or, if she did, she did so jokingly. Often her correspondents, especially her sister and brothers, only knew she had been ill because she told them she was better.

No doubt she had been trained from childhood to endure pain and hardship. 'You can go on', she said one day to Sister Cécile Pages who was 'blistering' her, 'I'm enured to pain . . . like cats'. But she was very far from deriving satisfaction from her sufferings; she had no desire to play the heroine. One day she said to a sister who asked if she prayed to her patron saint, Bernard, whose picture was by her bed: 'Oh yes, I pray to him but I do not imitate him. Saint Bernard liked suffering, but I avoid it if I can.' Bernadette in fact had a great zest for life; she was merry, roguish, even cunning at times; she enjoyed games, she liked tricks, and her biographers tell of her ruses to escape importunate visitors. One day a bishop visited her in the infirmary, and in order to procure a 'relic' he thought up the idea of letting his skull-cap fall onto the bed; she would give it back to him and thereby touch it. Sister Marie-Bernard, however, perceived his stratagem and didn't budge. 'Would you please pass me my skull-cap, Sister?' said the bishop. 'I didn't ask you for your skull-cap, Monsignor', said the girl, 'you can pick it up for yourself.' Unfortunately a superior was present and Sister Marie-Bernard had to relent.

Bernadette would have preferred active service to her 'job of being ill', as she called it. However, she set great store on such tasks as her health permitted her to do, from looking after sick sisters to making those albs of lace or crochet which have been preserved at Nevers and Lourdes. She certainly was not 'good for nothing' even if she was not as useful as she would have liked to be, and this was a not inconsiderable aspect of her physical suffering.

Her moral sufferings

Under this heading we shall deal with Bernadette's bereavements, her family relationships, the quarrels among historians concerning the events at Massabielle, and, last but not least, her relations with the Community.

First, *the bereavements*. Hardly had she arrived at Saint-Gildard than she lost her mother. Louise died on 8 December 1866, while the Vespers of the Immaculate Conception were being sung for the first time in the crypt of the Lourdes basilica. She was 41. Sister Marie-Bernard heard the news on 2 January 1867 and immediately wrote to Father Pomian: 'I could never have believed that such a tragic loss would strike at my heart so soon; it would be impossible to describe the pain I felt on hearing so unexpectedly of my mother's death; I heard of her death before I heard that she was ill . . . I went straight to offer this grievous sacrifice to Our Lord and his blessed Mother, and sought refuge at the foot of their altar to say a few prayers for the repose of her soul and to implore their help for the rest of my family. And while I was there I also asked Our Lord to be so good as to grant me the graces I needed to carry this cross courageously.'

On 2 September 1867 her sister, Toinette, married Joseph Sabathe, and the dreary toll of bereavements throughout the decade of the 'seventies started with the death of Toinette's first child in February 1871. In the March of that year François Soubirous died, and Bernadette wrote to Toinette: 'It has pleased Our Lord to take from us the dearest thing we had on earth, our dear and beloved father. So here I am, crying with you. But let us remain always submissive and resigned, however grieviously afflicted, to the paternal hand that has tried us sorely for some time now. Let us carry and embrace the cross that our dear Jesus gives us: let us ask him, and also the Most Blessed Virgin, for strength and courage to carry it as they did, without letting ourselves be crushed.' (ESB, 282.) And she wrote to her small brother of eleven, who was also her godchild: 'I'm sure that you have been deeply distressed by the loss of our beloved father who has been so suddenly taken from us. You had the happiness of seeing him a few days before he died – what a consolation for you, and for him too! I have thanked God for it. Let us also give him thanks for having allowed our dear departed to receive the Last Sacraments. Let us pray a great deal, my dear little Pierre, for the repose of his soul, and for those of our poor mother and of our dear aunt Lucile whom God has also called to himself. And do not forget in your prayers our good sister Marie [Toinette] who needs courage and health to look after her little boy. Her motherly heart has suffered deeply through the death of her little Bernadette.' (ESB, 284.)

In fact all five of Toinette's babies died. After the death of the fourth, on 12 August 1876, Bernadette wrote to her sister: 'I know that for a mother's heart it is a tragic, even a cruel blow to lose her fourth child; it is a bitter ordeal indeed . . . But I like to imagine that dear little group praying in heaven for us poor exiles on this miserable earth. Courage! – our family is more numerous in heaven than on earth. Let us pray, work and suffer for as long as Our Lord wants us to: in a little while perhaps we too shall share in their happiness. My good and dear Marie, I charge you to be reasonable, and Joseph too; don't give yourselves over to grief.' (ESB, 435.)

On 8 September 1877 Father Peyramale died, which elicited the following letter from Bernadette to Father Pomian: 'It is impossible to tell you, Father, what I have suffered! But the greater my pain, the sweeter was the consolation I felt in reading that our lamented Father had the joy of receiving the Last Sacraments with his full knowledge, and of having you beside him in his last moments – you, the friend of his heart, his faithful and zealous servant. The Most Blessed Virgin came to fetch our good Father on the day of her nativity.' (ESB, 490.) On 1 March 1878 Mother General Imbert died, and so the hollows were scooped out in Sister Marie-Bernard's life. It was on 28 February 1879 that Toinette's fifth child died at the age of eighteen months.

But it was not only bereavements that saddened these years. As the eldest of the Soubirous family Bernadette felt a deep responsibility for her two brothers, especially now that her mother and father were dead. Her brother Jean-Marie had entered the novitiate of the Ploermel Brothers early in 1871 and on the day he received his habit he even took the name of Brother Marie-Bernard. After his military service, however, his thoughts went in other directions, and in July 1876 Bernadette wrote to him: 'Tell me what you are thinking of doing, for you must know that I am as keenly interested in you from far away as from near. If I ask this question you surely realize that it is not from idle curiosity; no, my dear friend, as we no longer have our dear parents, it seems to me that it is my duty, as your elder sister, to watch over you, and it is unnecessary to tell you what a keen interest I take in all three of you. I must admit that at this moment I am very much concerned about your future, and about Pierre's. I pray every day to Our Lord and the Most Blessed Virgin to give you light.' (ESB, 429.)

In February 1877 Jean-Marie married. Bernadette's letter tells its own tale: 'Please don't think that I was cross because you had married, no, not at all, but it seems to me that it would have been more appropriate if I had heard about it two or three days before it happened; it would have been a joy for me to join my prayers with yours . . . I shall just whisper in your ear that I found your letter rather cold. As you tell me your wife's name, surely it would not have cost you too much to tell me if she comes from Lourdes, and especially if she comes from a Christian family. I hope, my

A first draft of the letter which Bernadette wrote to Pope Pius IX on 17 December 1876

Four pages from the scrap-book, measuring only 2½ x 4½", in which Bernadette wrote her innermost thoughts during her time in Nevers. Archives of the Convent of Saint Gildard in Nevers

The sick room in the Convent of Saint Gildard. Far right is Bernadette's bed, which, during the time she suffered from tuberculosis of the bones, she often called 'my white chapel'

In the Chapel of Joseph, in the convent garden of Saint Gildard – destroyed by bombs in 1944, but since rebuilt – Bernadette, who had died on 16 April 1879, found her last resting place. Thirty years later her earthly remains were exhumed and found to be 'whole and without any signs of decay'

The stream of pilgrims and sick people to the Grotto at Lourdes and its miraculous source began soon after the appearances; in 1866 the crypt of the basilica above the Grotto was consecrated. Father Lambert sent Bernadette this engraving in 1868

Bishop Bertrand-Sévère Laurence of Tarbes led the church enquiry into the appearances in the Grotto of Massabielle, and on 18 January 1862 gave permission for church ceremonies at the Grotto

Overleaf The face of the saint to whom the Lady in the Grotto had said, 'I do not promise to make you happy in this world, but rather in the other'

Bernadette in the habit of the Sisters of Nevers (1866)

dear friend, that you will write a little more warmly next time.' (ESB, 476.)

In fact in December 1878 Jean-Marie went to visit her at Nevers, their first encounter for twelve years. Despite the misunderstandings that had occurred, the meeting was a very affectionate one, but Jean-Marie departed with no illusion as to his sister's health.

Bernadette's younger brother, Pierre, also decided not to become a priest, and she wrote to him as follows on 3 November 1876: 'I have been told that you probably won't be going back to Garaison this year. If you truly think that God is not calling you to the religious life, then I urge you with all my heart to decide to learn some decent trade. I urge you, my dear brother, to stand before God and think very hard. I wouldn't for the world want you to become a priest so as to have a good position; no, I would rather you became a rag-and-bone man. I hope you will understand that it's only my concern for your soul that makes me speak like this. Once again, pray and think and ask Our Lord and the Most Blessed Virgin to let you know their blessed will.' (ESB, 445.)

Toinette and her husband Joseph, Jean-Marie and his wife and Pierre all lived under the same roof at Lourdes, and on 17 July 1877 Bernadette, having heard of family quarrels, wrote as follows: 'I'm ashamed of all of you. What must the townspeople be thinking of you when you squabble among yourselves? You, who should be giving a good example? I am really feeling most distressed at the thought of the disharmony among you.'

A month before Bernadette died, on 18 March 1879, she had the joy of a visit from Toinette and Joseph.

The next of her sufferings under this heading were caused by the *quarrels among historians*.

We have already had a glimpse of the gruelling cross-examinations Bernadette had to undergo at Lourdes, and the sceptical gibes of which she was the victim – from people of every kind, including churchmen. But at Nevers this sort of thing became worse.

Towards the end of 1867 the *Revue du Monde Catholique* published the first of a series of articles by Henri Lasserre from which his book, *Our Lady of Lourdes*, was to be made. Early in February 1868 he sent the first part of his book to Mother Superior at Nevers with instructions that it shouldn't be shown to Sister Marie-Bernard. However, there was a delay in its publication, the public became impatient, and two priests, Fathers Sempé and Duboé, undertook to write *A Short History of the Appearances* which they brought out in *Annales*. This prompted an extremely irate Henri Lasserre to hurry to Nevers, question Sister Marie-Bernard, collect from her a few criticisms of the *Short History*, draw up a *Protest* and get her to sign it. Father Sempé did not take long to react. He hurried to Nevers in his turn, questioned Sister Marie-Bernard, drew up a *Counter-Protest* but, out of pity for the invalid, did not ask her to sign it. In the course of these interviews, which dealt with tiny details (as Father Laurentin has pointed out), an anxiety took root in Bernadette's mind: she noticed that there were certain facts that had totally vanished from her memory, and that she was unable to provide the details that seemed so important to her learned visitors. 'It's all long ago . . . very long ago . . . all those things, I don't remember them too well, and I don't like talking about them, for, oh my God, just supposing I was mistaken . . .'

Another ordeal was lying in wait for Bernadette right at the end of her life – it lasted from 25 August 1878 until 3 March 1879. Father Leonard Cros, a Jesuit and an intrepid and pitiless researcher, had been asked by the chaplains at Lourdes to write a scientific history of the appearances, and his superiors had given their consent to the project. Such a man, motivated by obedience and an absolute respect for truth, was not going to let any obstacle stand in his way. In 1877 and 1878 he conducted a large-scale inquiry at Lourdes among 200 witnesses of the Event. All that remained was for him to interview Bernadette herself. On 25 June 1878 he wrote to the Bishop of Nevers 'for permission to obtain from Sister Marie-Bernard the necessary information for a new work on the Appearances and Sister Marie-Bernard's life. (ESB,468.) The bishop, in consultation with Mother Superior, refused. On 25 August Cros, undaunted, turned up at Saint-Gildard but again was refused: Sister Marie-Bernard had been promised that no-one would question her any more and that neither would she be 'produced' as heretofore. Father Cros appealed to Rome, and with the help of an intermediary, Monsignor Langenieux, Archbishop of Reims, he obtained a Brief from Leo XIII who declared himself 'indebted to any one who would help to bring the project to a satisfactory conclusion'. Very well, said the Sisters, but someone must be chosen by the Bishop of Tarbes to interview Bernadette instead of Father Cros. The man chosen was Father Sempé who, armed with questions prepared by Father Cros, presented himself at Saint-Gildard where he interrogated Sister Marie-Bernard for two days (12–13 December 1878). The results were disappointing regarding new material though they confirmed the former accounts. To many questions Sister Marie-Bernard answered: 'I don't remember', but on essential points she remained faithful to what she had said in 1858. This did not satisfy Father Cros. He wanted to know more. He despatched further questionnaires to Nevers – on 31 December, 28 January and 19 February. In sending him Sister Marie-Bernard's answers on 3 March the Mother

Superior made it clear that she would not interrogate the invalid any more. 'It pains me a great deal to have to bother her. She cannot understand why people have to come back over and over again when the Ecclesiastical Commission [of Tarbes] wrote everything down at her dictation at the time of the event.' (ESB, 469.)

It is in this context that Bernadette made her famous remark: 'The best thing is for people to write very simply – it is more moving to read the Passion than to have it explained.'

In discussing Sister Marie-Bernard's *relations with the Community* at Saint-Gildard, it has to be said that they were on the whole very good. If the Sisters closed the convent doors to her followers, this was in accordance with the prudent policy inaugurated by Father Peyramale and Mayor Lacadé at Lourdes, and in any case Bernadette had entered the convent to 'hide' – this was her deepest spiritual wish.

But despite the anonymity which she sought and was helped to find, she was surrounded by affection. 'In the novitiate everyone spoils me', she wrote to Mother Ceyrac on 3 September 1866, and to her aunt Bernarde on 27 December 1876, 'It is not care that I lack: I am quite embarrassed by all the kindnesses I receive from my superiors and companions.' (ESB, 471.)

But Bernadette was not without faults. Let us look at a few of her characteristics as they appear in the somewhat elliptical notes that were kept of an interview between Father Febvre, the Mother Superior and the Mother Secretary: 'Merry . . . sudden outbursts of good spirits, especially when she was well . . . Sudden changes of mood and unevenness of temper – this a divine intervention, perhaps, to secure her against too strong affections from outside: she would have been spoilt. Unsociability regarding visits from outside . . . very good at making excuses: it is probable that God allowed those faults (bouts of bad temper) to provide an occasion for acts of humility. Very active, could not bear being idle even in her sick-bed, always work of some kind in her hands' (Father Febvre). 'Inclination to stubbornness; opinionated. She was not demonstrative of affection – this was a grace of her mission . . . Her character was more at one with itself when she was ill . . . She dreaded visits. But gracious enough when face to face. You had to do the rounds of the whole Community to find her. She fled like a mouse. Once there, she made a nice curtsy and obliged.' (the Mother Superior and the Mother Secretary.)

It is in this context that we should quote some of the directives given her by another convent chaplain, Father Douce, as they occur in her retreat notes: 'Remember what the Blessed Virgin said to you: "Penance! Penance!" You should be the first to put it into practice. So suffer in silence all that comes to you from your companions for this intention, that Jesus and Mary may be glorified' (September 1874). 'In your last retreat I counselled you to keep yourself hidden, following Mary's example. From now you will keep yourself still more hidden, with her, at the foot of the cross. You will accept all that comes to you from your companions and your superiors as if it came from Our Lord. Remember the Blessed Virgin's words: "Penance! Penance!" Suffer everything in silence for this intention, for sinners' (July 1875).

The above would seem to indicate that friction was not unknown between Sister Marie-Bernard and the òther members of the Community, an impression strengthened by a note in 1874: 'I must fight my dominant fault: touchiness.'

Yet the three sisters with whom she worked in the sacristy and the infirmary in 1874 and 1875, and with whom her relations were most likely to be prickly, showed no hint of either reserve or aggression when preparing depositions for the canonization proceedings.

As for Bernadette's superiors, we know that Mother Superior Imbert could be ironical at her expense when she so wished, yet the letter that Bernadette wrote her when she was in Rome in 1870 tells its own story: 'For a long time my heart has felt the need to write to you, but ever since you left I have been almost always either laid up myself or looking after our dear invalids.. . . As for myself, I developed an abscess in my mouth which became inflamed and caused me a lot of pain. I am up again now though my mouth is still crooked. I do not fail to offer all the small sacrifices and sufferings that God sends me for your intentions . . . I do not forget in my prayers, feeble as they are, all the people you were good enough to commend to my attention before you left, it is especially on the days when I receive Communion that I acquit myself of the debt, I feel my soul is full of strength and confidence because I think it is no longer myself who am praying but Jesus within me. I pray very particularly for the needs of the Council and of our Order and for our Holy Father the Pope.' (ESB, 278.)

It was the relations between Sister Marie-Bernard and the novice-mistress, Mother Vauzou, that are known to have been difficult. These two were different from each other as to temperament, background and education, and even their spiritual graces – rich as these were in both of them – were out of harmony. Mother Vauzou treated her novice to sharp words, bitter sarcasm, hurtful outbursts and painful humiliations. These, according to Mother Vauzou's confidential report on Bernadette, were in order to conquer her two main faults: obstinacy and touchiness. It must be said that Mother Vauzou added to this report that her novice was 'modest, pious, devout and orderly'. It must also be remembered that Father Peyramale himself had recommended a degree of severity towards Bernadette on the part of the Sisters of Nevers so that she should not be lost 'through pride'.

However, when asked whether Mother Vauzou's methods had caused her to feel resentment, Bernadette replied with feeling, 'Oh no, she is quite right, because I'm very proud; but now I'm here I shall work at correcting this'. A sister tells the story (though this concerns the Mother Superior) that one day she and Bernadette were both going from the novice room up to the infirmary, because the sister had been unwell for some days: 'On the way we met Mother Superior who, no doubt wanting to test us, addressed us as "useless members of the community". I started to cry. "You cry for so little", Bernadette said. "Cheer up; it'll often happen again!"'

Bernadette's ordeal with the Community must be seen in perspective. It may certainly have had repercussions on her deep spiritual ordeal, but the two must not be confused. It was in the very depths of her being that, as Father Febvre put it, Bernadette was really 'worked on' by God.

Her spiritual sufferings

Perhaps Bernadette's greatest anguish on the spiritual plane was her fear of not responding adequately to the graces she had been given. We get our first glimpse of this in a letter she wrote to Don Antonio Moralis as early as 3 December 1862: 'I beseech you to ask our good Mother, the Most Blessed Virgin Immaculate, to obtain from her divine Son the grace to respond faithfully to all God's designs on me. I am very weak; I have great need of the help of good people's prayers so as not to betray the favour I received from Heaven, unworthy as I was.'

The theme recurs in Bernadette's letter of 2 May 1864 to Mother Ursule Fardes: 'It is a great happiness for me to have this opportunity of talking to you, but I would be happier still if God would grant me the grace to see you for a moment. My poor heart would have many things to say to you; all I can say on this piece of paper is to ask you to have the charity to pray for me, for my need is great.'

When she wrote to Mother Ursule on 18 June 1866 to tell her she was entering the Order of the Sisters of Nevers, she asked her to pray to Our Lord 'that I shall be a holy nun and respond to the graces God is giving me.' (ESB, 190.)

Bernadette's secret anxiety followed her to Nevers. On 21 August 1866 she wrote to the Bishop of Tarbes to say: 'I need help and grace if I am to respond to the countless favours I have received from Our Lord

. . . I am more and more aware of my impotence, especially since having the happiness to receive the sacred habit. This, added to the beautiful names so dear to my heart of Marie-Bernard, imposes enormous debts on me.'

In November 1868 Father Peyramale wrote Sister Marie-Bernard a letter containing significant advice: 'Your mission at the Grotto is over, so now you must work at your sanctification, live the hidden life in Jesus Christ, show God your gratitude for all the favours he has granted you by leading an exemplary life in the holy house that has taken you in and where you are surrounded by so much kindness.' (ESB, 275.)

✳ In 1871 Sister Marie-Bernard copied out an 'Act of perfect Love for the general acceptance of all crosses'. Though its origin has not been traced it certainly meant a great deal to her, for she transcribed it carefully on a large sheet of paper whereas usually she used cheap exercise-books for her notes and jottings. 'I shall bless you and give you thanks . . . for the discomforts and pains of the body, and for the afflictions of the spirit and the heart. I shall accept everything from your divine hand and for your love, knowing that an infinitely good Father cannot bring suffering to his children except to save them.'

As far as we can judge by the documents at our disposal, the year 1873 brought an intensification of Sister Marie-Bernard's spiritual ordeal as well as of her physical one, Her cousin, Lucile Pène, had written to tell her that the family was praying for her, knowing how ill she was. 'Thank you for the prayers that you and your dear parents are offering for me', she replied; 'pray less for my health and a great deal for my poor soul; ask Our Lord to make me after his heart, ask him often. I shall always have sufficient health, but never enough love for Our Lord.' (ESB, 321.)

These letters make us hungry to know more, and here Sister Marie-Bernard's 'spiritual notes' come to our assistance, though this expression should not raise our hopes unduly. We are not dealing here with a Journal of the Soul but with an anthology of texts that she copied out in little notebooks and on odd bits of paper. Though these texts are not *by* her, strictly speaking, they nevertheless reveal her because she chose them. There are also jottings of her own about retreats, about directives from Father Douce received in the confessional, prayers, and so on; but for the most part Sister Marie-Bernard shows herself to be one of those 'spiritual bees', referred to by St Francis of Sales, who go from flower to flower to gather the juice that makes their honey.

Certain spiritual tendencies stand out clearly enough from these notes: first and foremost a passionate and very personal love for Jesus and Jesus crucified, an exclusive love demanding the total gift of self, if it was to be sincere. Sometimes there appears the word 'victim', but not over-insistently, rather in its right theological context. The Blessed Virgin of course is there, though, curiously, the expression Immaculate Conception is very seldom used; rather Mary or My Mother. A typical text is one she copied out on a holy picture entitled 'The Fiat of the Children of Mary'. It reads: 'Through love of Jesus I shall do violence to my feelings at every opportunity.' The resonance of the Gospel phrase 'It was necessary for Christ to suffer so as to enter into his glory' vibrates through all these pages.

The climax of Bernadette's private notes, and the passage which best reveals her spiritual drama, is an astonishing text on Our Lord's 'abandonments'. Fortunately we have found the source of this quotation in a 1580 Portuguese work by Father Thomas of Jesus: 'The Sufferings of Our Lord Jesus Christ.' We wonder how and why Sister Marie-Bernard went to fetch this book from the convent library. Here is the text:

O Jesus, desolate and at the same time refuge of desolate souls, your love teaches me that it is from your abandonments that I must draw the strength I need to endure my own. I know that the most terrible abandonment into which I could fall would be to have no part in yours. But as you have given me life through your death, and have delivered me, through your suffering, from the suffering that was my due, so you have also obtained, through your forsakenness, that the heavenly Father should not forsake me, and that he should never be nearer to me, through his mercy, than when I am most united to you through his desolation of me.

O Jesus, light of my soul, illumine my inner eyes in time of tribulation, and, as it is necessary for me to undergo it, have no regard for my fears and my weakness.

O my God, I do not ask you not to afflict me through your abandonments, but not to abandon me in my affliction; rather, teach me to seek you in it as my only consoler, to strengthen my faith, to fortify my hope, to purify my love; give me the grace to recognize your hand in my affliction and not to want any consoler but you.

Then humiliate me as much as you please, and console me only so that I may be able to suffer and persevere until death, in suffering. As the graces that I ask of you are the fruit of your abandonments, let their virtue appear in my weakness, and glorify yourself in my wretchedness, O my Jesus, sole refuge of my soul.

O most blessed Mother of my Jesus, you who saw and felt the uttermost desolation of your dear Son, help me when the time comes for mine.

And you, saints of Paradise, who have passed through that ordeal, have compassion on those who suffer, and obtain for me the grace to remain faithful until death. (ESB, 350–1.)

This passage on Our Lord's abandonments, combined with other quotations in her private notebooks, throw light on Sister Marie-Bernard's own writings as her life drew to a close, and on her death itself. Here, for instance, is what she wrote to her cousin, Jeanne Védère, on her decision to become a Cistercian nun: 'No need to tell you the joy I felt on hearing that Our Lord had at last answered your prayers . . . I seem to see you now hungering for the cross and for sufferings, so as to show him your love and gratitude.' (ESB, 391.)

And here is her letter to Pope Pius IX taken to Rome by the Bishop of Nevers in December 1876:

> What can I do, Most Holy Father, to show you my deep gratitude? . . . My weapons are prayer and sacrifice which I shall use until my last breath. Only then shall the weapon of sacrifice be laid down, but the weapon of prayer will follow me to heaven, where it will be much more powerful than in our exile on earth. I pray every day to the Sacred Heart of Jesus and the Immaculate Heart of Mary to keep you in the midst of us for a long time yet, for you have made them known and loved so well. Every time I pray according to your intentions, it seems to me that the Most Blessed Virgin, from heaven, must often turn her eyes on you, Most Holy Father, as you proclaimed her immaculate and, four years later, this good Mother came to earth to say: I am the Immaculate. I did not know what that meant, I had never heard this word. Since then I have thought to myself that the Blessed Virgin is good: it would seem that she came to confirm our Holy Father's words . . .

This letter shows the place at the heart of the Church that Bernadette felt called upon to occupy since the events of Massabielle – she must pray and suffer according to the intentions of the Vicar of Christ. Indeed this is the vocation of everyone who, through baptism, has been drawn into the death and resurrection of Christ and who is a member of his Mystical Body. Like all Christians, Saint Bernadette was called to live the mystery of Christ within the stuff of existence. Her religious vows made her, in the words of the liturgy, a 'bride of Christ'. To this call of love she gave herself in all simplicity, 'without ifs or buts or conditions', as she put it in the words of St Jeanne Chantal (ESB, 507). 'She was more worked on than working', said Father Febvre, and rightly (ESB, 515). And when a soul gives itself totally to Love in this way, the Father treats it rather as he treated his own Son: 'Yes, it's very painful not to be able to breathe', said Sister Marie-Bernard to Sister Julie Garros in 1875 after an acute attack of

Right View over the Gave towards the Basilique du Rosaire, which was completed in 1872, and which stands over the Grotto of Massabielle in Lourdes

Overleaf Solemn procession on the occasion of the 25th anniversary of the first appearance in 1883, from the Grotto of Massabielle to the completed basilica of Lourdes. A picture not on show to the public in the Bernadette Museum in Saint Gildard at Nevers

asthma, 'but it is much more painful being tortured by interior anguish. This is terrible.' For Christ, too, the agony in the garden was a harsher passion than the cross on Calvary, or rather the former gave its full meaning to the latter.

How much further can we penetrate into Bernadette's spiritual life? There are some texts that give us a pointer. Ever since Massabielle, 'sinners' had been present in Bernadette's prayers and sacrifices. But though she sometimes saw sinners as distinct from herself, as in this prayer: 'Accept each of my tears, each of my groans, as a supplication for the suffering, the sorrowful, and those who forget you', and in her remark to Mother Ursule Fardes, 'Sinners are, after all, our brothers', yet there was something much deeper than this: she identified herself with sinners, she herself was one of them. In the manual of the devout life in use at Nevers there was a section dealing with preparation for death in which the Hail Mary was thus modified: 'Holy Mary, Mother of God, pray for me, poor sinner, now and at the hour of my death', and it is hardly surprising that these words came to Bernadette's lips at her own death. But she emphasized and underlined the two words 'poor sinner' with an insistence that shows to what point she had made them her own even before her death. The gentle Hail Mary of Massabielle had become the prayer of her personal torment. And this torment arose, as far as we can see, from two causes: her sense of never being able to repay the kindnesses of those around her, and her sense of never being able to respond to the graces received from God. 'I am afraid', she said. 'I have received so many graces, and profited from them so little.' (ESB, 512.)

Bernadette's Death – 'Ground Like a Grain of Wheat'

'The Christian life does not consist only of its struggles and its trials', wrote Sister Marie-Bernard in her notebook, 'for if we have to go from Tabor to Calvary, we also come back from Calvary to Tabor with Jesus.' The moment came for her to make this mystical journey for the last time.

On 30 October 1878 the infirmary for the professed nuns had been transferred to premises named Sainte-Croix. It was here that Sister Marie-Bernard lived her slow agony and died. A year earlier, on hearing

Left A recent photograph of a candlelit procession of pilgrims and the sick in front of the basilica of Lourdes

of Father Peyramale's death, she had written: 'Oh, now it will soon be my turn, but before that I must die another death.' When she drew her last breath she was so stripped, so reduced, so annihilated, that it almost seemed as if she did die a death before dying.

On 28 March 1879, the Friday before Passion Sunday, Father Febvre gave Bernadette the last sacraments for the fourth time. She received them with eager faith. 'At the moment of receiving Holy Communion', relates the Mother Superior, 'her voice became so distinct that everyone was astonished – I think it was because she saw me in the distance' – the Mother Superior had arrived late on tiptoe and was at some distance from the sick-bed. 'My dear Mother', said Sister Marie-Bernard, 'I beg your forgiveness for all the sorrow I have caused you and for all my failures to keep the Rule, and I beg forgiveness from my dear sisters for the bad example I have given them, especially through my pride.' She spoke 'with an accent of conviction that astonished everyone, like a preacher who wants to make himself heard', noted the Mother Secretary. (ESB, 518.)

Holy week was a time of great suffering for Sister Marie-Bernard. Although she was so steadfast in face of pain, she could not help letting out groans during her 'terrible attacks'. 'Oh please forgive me, Sister', she said to her nurse, 'for moaning like this'. (ESB, 517.) It was a week marked by significant renunciations. She asked that all her pictures hanging around her 'white chapel', as she called her cubicle, be removed, including the picture of her patron saint, Bernard, which she had brought with her from Lourdes. Only her crucifix remained, the crucifix sent her by Pius IX in answer to her letter of 17 September 1876. 'It is enough', she said.

It was on Easter Monday, 14 April, that she said to Sister Léontine the famous phrase redolent of her happy childhood at the mill: 'I am ground like a grain of wheat.' During the night of Monday/Tuesday 'she entered into a sort of agony', relates Mother Bordenave, and she was heard to say several times, 'Go away, Satan'. 'On Tuesday morning', explains Father Febvre, 'she told me that the devil had tried to frighten her and she had invoked the sacred Name of Jesus and all had vanished.' The Father exhorted her to renew the sacrifice of her life,' continues Mother Bordenave. 'What sacrifice?' asked Bernadette 'it is no sacrifice to leave a poor world where one suffers so much in serving God.' One of the nuns around her said: 'Are you suffering a great deal, Sister?' To which she replied: 'All this is good for heaven.' 'I'm going to ask our Immaculate Mother to give you consolation.' 'No, no, not consolation, but strength and patience.'

Towards seven o'clock at night one of her best friends, Sister Nathalie

Portat, came to visit her, and it was then that Bernadette made the remark quoted above: 'I am afraid; I have received so many graces, and profited from them so little.' Sister Nathalie promised her that she would 'give thanks to the Blessed Virgin right to the end'. 'Oh thank you', said the invalid.

Towards half past eleven in the morning of the day of her death, the Wednesday of Easter week, 16 April 1879, she asked to get up and was therefore moved to an armchair. At one o'clock the chaplain was urgently summoned. 'She was seated in the armchair, hardly breathing, and suffering the most cruel pain. She made her confession with edifying fervour.' Then, remembering the special blessing that Pius IX had granted her for the hour of her death, she asked for the rescript, thinking she had to hold it in her hands for the favour to be applicable. She was told that invocation of the name of Jesus, accompanied by an intention, would suffice. 'In order not to be separated from her crucifix that she could no longer hold, she asked for it to be fastened on her breast.' Mother Eléonore Cassagnes said: 'My dear Sister, you are properly on the cross.' She stretched out her arms to the crucifix hanging on the wall and said: 'My Jesus, Oh! how I love you.' The prayers for the dying were recited around her and she made the responses 'in a faint but clear voice'.

'An hour before her death', according to Mother Bordenave's account, 'she raised her eyes towards heaven, and they gazed for some time at a fixed point; her face breathed calm, serenity and I know not what grave melancholy; then, with an indefinable expression that showed surprise rather then pain, she cried: "Oh! Oh! Oh!" At the same time her whole body shook. She let her trembling hand fall on her heart, her eyes fell, and in a clear voice she said: "My God, I love you with my whole heart, with my whole soul, with my whole strength!"'

Now let her friend and confidant, Sister Nathalie Portat, take up the story. (ESB, 513.) 'Towards three o'clock in the afternoon she seemed in the grip of inexpressible interior anguish. The sisters in the infirmary were alarmed and fetched holy water which they sprinkled over her while suggesting pious invocations to her. She took hold of her crucifix, contemplated it with love, then slowly kissed Christ's wounds, one by one. It was at this moment that Sister X [this was how Sister Nathalie referred to herself] came into the infirmary and drew close to Bernadette who seemed absorbed in the contemplation of her crucifix. Suddenly she raised her head, held her arms out towards Sister X, and said, "My dear Sister, forgive me . . . pray for me . . . pray for me."

'Sister X and two nurses knelt down. The dying woman united herself to their intentions which she repeated in a low voice . . . Then she raised her eyes towards heaven, held out her arms in the shape of a cross and said: "My God!" . . . At last she let her arms fall and again joined in the prayers of her companions. At the words, Holy Mary, Mother of God, her animation returned . . . as she twice repeated: "Holy Mary, Mother of God, pray for me, poor sinner, poor sinner . . ."

'Death was approaching . . . The dying woman gazed mutely at Sister X, her arms outstretched. Sister X tried to interpret the questioning look in her eyes, and when she said, "It's so that you'll help me", Sister X remembered her promise of the day before "to help her give thanks to the Blessed Virgin right to the end . . ." Some moments later the invalid gestured for something to drink; she made the sign of the cross, took hold of the flask offered her, swallowed a few drops twice over, lowered her head, and gently drew her last breath. It was three o'clock, the hour when Christ died on the cross for the glory of his father.'

'The Rock I Love So Much'

When in 1866 Mother Vauzou told the novices of Saint-Gildard that Bernadette would soon be joining them, she could not hide her joy at the thought of seeing 'the eyes that had seen the Blessed Virgin'. We can savour something of this joy still today when we look at Bernadette in her glass coffin. The eyes are shut, but she is still there. Intact is the face on which the marvellous light of the mystery of the Virgin still glows; intact are the lips which moved during the dialogue between the Lady and the child; intact are the hands which, on Aquerò's instructions, scratched the earth at Massabielle and discovered the miraculous spring; intact is the brave and tender heart that beat with love for Jesus Christ and for Mary his Mother, and, because of them, for all the sinners of the world; intact is Bernadette, just as if she was asleep and waiting for the Angel's call to rise.

When writing from Nevers to her friends in Lourdes, Bernadette told them she would meet them at Massabielle: 'It is there that you will find me, close to the Rock I love so much.' Massabielle, Nevers it is all one.

The Rock for us today is still Massabielle, but it is also that body intact in its shrine. Rock of faith, of fidelity and love! Rock of light in the depth of our darkness! O stone enshrined at the heart of the Church!

Bibliography

Books Quoted in the Text

ANDL = *Annales de Notre-Dame de Lourdes*
ESB   = A. Ravier and Saint Gildard Convent: *Les Ecrits de Sainte Bernadette et sa voie spirituelle,* 1961

Other Books on Bernadette Soubirous

Franz Werfel: *The Song of Bernadette,* Fontana, London, 1958 and Avon Books, New York, 1975

Frances Parkinson Keyes: *Bernadette of Lourdes,* A. Clarke Books, London, 1975 and Westminster Press, Philadelphia

René Laurentin: *Bernadette of Lourdes,* Winston, Minneapolis, 1979

Calendar of the Appearances, 1858

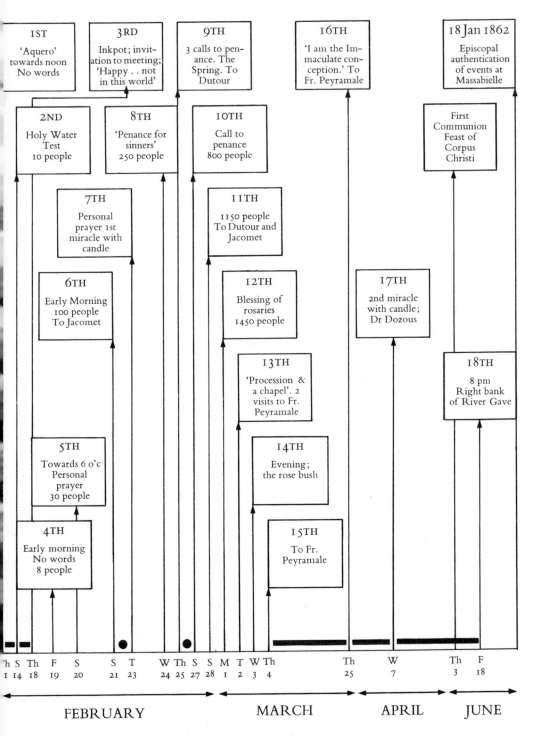

1ST	3RD	9TH	16TH	18 Jan 1862
'Aquero' towards noon No words	Inkpot; invitation to meeting; 'Happy . . not in this world'	3 calls to penance. The Spring. To Dutour	'I am the Immaculate conception.' To Fr. Peyramale	Episcopal authentication of events at Massabielle

2ND — Holy Water Test 10 people

8TH — 'Penance for sinners' 250 people

10TH — Call to penance 800 people

First Communion Feast of Corpus Christi

7TH — Personal prayer 1st miracle with candle

11TH — 1150 people To Dutour and Jacomet

6TH — Early Morning 100 people To Jacomet

12TH — Blessing of rosaries 1450 people

17TH — 2nd miracle with candle; Dr Dozous

13TH — 'Procession & a chapel'. 2 visits to Fr. Peyramale

18TH — 8 pm Right bank of River Gave

5TH — Towards 6 o'c Personal prayer 30 people

14TH — Evening; the rose bush

4TH — Early morning No words 8 people

15TH — To Fr. Peyramale

'h S Th   F   S   S   T   W Th S S M T W Th   Th   W   Th   F
1 14 18   19   20   21 23   24 25 27 28 1 2 3 4   25   7   3   18

FEBRUARY   MARCH   APRIL   JUNE

● ▬▬   DAY OR PERIOD WITHOUT APPEARANCES